TOURISM, BIODIVERSITY
AND
SUSTAINABLE DEVELOPMENT

TOURISM, BIODIVERSITY AND SUSTAINABLE DEVELOPMENT

(In 6 Volumes)

New Directives in Hospitality and Tourism

(Volume 4)

Editor

Prof. O.P. KANDARI

ASHISH CHANDRA

ISHA BOOKS

DELHI—110 033

Tourism, Biodiversity and Sustainable Development
(Tourism/Culture)

Rs. 5000 (Set in 6 Vols.)
Rs. 850 (Each Volume)

ISBN: 81-8205-033-2 (Set)
ISBN: 81-8205-037-5 (Vol. 4)

Published in 2004 in India by
Isha Books, D-43, Prithviraj Road
Adarsh Nagar, Delhi-110 033

Lasertypesetting by: Varsha Graphics, Delhi
Printed at: Chawla Offset Press, Delhi

Contents

Preface

Tourism is a unique industry that is growing rapidly and under some measures may now be the world's largest industry. It is very sensitive to changes in the economic, social or environmental conditions of a destination. Tourists bring foreign exchange, which can stimulate local economies through direct employment, purchase of goods, and multipliers such as service jobs, suppliers and home industries. While tourism may be an important source of economic benefits, continuing leakage of foreign exchange can greatly reduce net benefits to host nations.

The hospitality business is a massive industry encompassing all forms of transport, tourism, accommodation, eating, drinking, entertainment, recreation and activities. It is the world's largest employer of people and a vast consumer of physical resources. These days, the services or products offered to the modern traveller by hospitality establishments can cater for every human comfort.

Tourism and hospitality industries have a number of specific characteristics that challenge managers and the provision of appropriate governance. Management of both the fields remains problematic for national and local governments. Both the industries involve a range of services and uses resources traditionally managed by specific sectors. Management of these industries requires flexibility and the use of innovative solutions to deal with the range of effects unique to the industries.

The book endeavours to cover the planning, organisational and operational aspects of tourism and hospitality industries. It will be highly useful for practical guidance to all those who are keenly interested to have in-depth knowledge of this fast growing industries.

Editor

1

Globalisation and New Directions in Hospitality and Tourism

Tourism industry and the hotel has been suffering particularly from the combined effects of a general economic downturn that began to show itself early in 2001 and the shock wave from the events on September 11th of the same year. The general economic downturn had already started to reduce the industry's previously strong 4½ per cent annual growth rate to well below 4 per cent.

The impact of the September 11 th events on tourism was dramatic. The whole industry lost an additional 10 per cent or more of its business worldwide, with certain countries experiencing falls of up to 30 per cent. The extreme market lows remained for at least three months, plunging the industry's growth rate for the whole year 2001 into negative territory of somewhere between -1 per cent and -5 per cent.

Although signs of a recovery have been observed since January 2002, it is proving slow to take hold. More recent events have raised new security concerns worldwide. They include the terrorist attacks in Bali, 12 October, and in Mombasa, 14 November 2002. The Moscow hostage drama, late October, also contributes to an increased feeling of insecurity in the international sphere as does the perspective of a possibly aggravating conflict in the Middle East.

Recent reports, however, of the renewed decline in the third quarter of 2002 of certain performance indicators, suggest that a longer recovery period is to be expected. A flat performance, i. e. continued stagnation, now seems more likely. Longer-term predictions now suggest that the industry's pre-2001 growth rates will not be regained before the year 2004 and that it will take the market until 2005 to get back to its - outstanding - year 2000 volume.

Employment figures in the sector have reacted more slowly to the crisis, but the negative effects will be longer lasting. The common tendency, particularly in the service sectors, is for staff lay-offs to be partially compensated by increased productivity. Consequently, the longer the crisis lasts, or the slower the industry recovers, the more jobs are lost irretrievably.

According to estimates by the World Travel and Tourism Council (WTTC), the events of September 11 th and subsequent developments will have caused more than six and a half million jobs to be lost in the travel and tourism industry over the years 2001 and 2002 - some 6.9% of the total employed, as compared to a normal growth that could have been expected in normal times without the impact of a crisis. This estimate does not include those related sectors providing inputs to travel and tourism, where employment may have suffered in similar proportions.

Although international tourism is generally highlighted for statistical convenience, the crisis has had an important impact on domestic tourism levels as well, particularly in the United States, where much of the internal tourism involves the use of air transport. Both international and domestic tourism tend to reflect the general level consumer confidence.

Travel and tourism are the types of product on which consumers can easily make substantial savings if they need to, e.g. by purchasing lower quality services, by taking shorter leave or by spending their vacations closer to home. Adjustments like this have undoubtedly been made by consumers in order to adapt to the present increased economic and psychological pressures on travelling.

Nevertheless, there have been some initial signs of recovery in leisure tourism as can be observed in tour operators' business in early 2002. These signs serve, in a way, to illustrate both the extent to which leisure tourism suffered immediately following September 11 th and the fact that the crisis phase immediately thereafter in this particular sector seemed actually to be quite short.

One contributing factor might have been that the promotional campaigns undertaken by the tourism industry to mitigate the negative effects of the crisis, accompanied by measures taken to support small enterprises. They have also had a much greater effect on leisure tourism than on business travel. However, general economic constraints continue to force consumers to apply various types of savings measures such as avoiding air transport, choosing cheaper destinations, staying for shorter periods of time, and booking late.

Another point worth noting is that developing countries are not benefiting proportionately from any recovery in leisure tourism because of their heavy dependence on foreign tourists, and particularly on long-haul tourists. Business travel is recovering more slowly, if at all. Corporate travel professionals are not expecting to see a recovery in business travel for at least another year.

Although in terms of numbers, business travellers may account for no more than one-fifth of the total travelling population, they contribute nearly one-half of the industry's total revenue because of their high frequency of travel. It has been observed that, in light of the economic downturn, travel managers of corporations and businesses are moving to re-negotiate contracts in order to reduce business travel costs.

Most affected countries have taken measures on a central, regional or local level, aimed at mitigating the effects of the tourism crisis. To varying degrees, losses in long-haul international tourism have been successfully compensated by gains in international tourism from within a region. This is the case, for example, with certain European countries and with Canada, and some therefore ended the year 2001 registering positive growth in their levels of international tourism.

Domestic tourism in many developed countries benefited from reduced outbound tourism because many clients who were previously long-haul tourists now favour surface travel, and cheaper, shorter trips. Major and, at times, remarkable measures were taken to stimulate consumer demand and support the industry by sectoral bodies, including national tourist boards and ad hoc committees composed of tourism authorities and industry representatives in public-private partnerships.

Governments have been participating financially in advertising campaigns, quality improvement programmes, tax relief schemes, or the granting of subsidies to small and medium-sized enterprises (SME's). Despite the fact that the developments in tourism after 11 September 2002 are those of a crisis with a beginning and hopefully with an end, they seem to have introduced or at least accelerated lasting changes in consumer demand for tourism products.

New trends show an inclination to stay closer to home and make sure that holidays are an "experience," be it in the area of cultural enrichment, in the area of sport or other. Providers are challenged to meet those specific types of demand by developing higher value products and at the same time compensate a tendency of consumers to spend less money.

Developing countries are particularly challenged in order to compensate for long distance travel, language differences, and less complete infrastructure to receive tourists other than in beach resorts. For most countries, knowledge of the volume of border crossing tourism is largely limited to the numbers of arrivals and the expenditure by international tourists in the host country published with varying delay by governments and presented annually by the World Tourism Organization (WTO).

Some more frequent statistical surveys are carried out based on samples covering also domestic tourism and especially hotel performance indicators, but these do not produce figures representative of the total size of the industry. Only a dozen countries have so far started to develop statistical instruments to measure the whole tourist industry (Tourism Satellite Accounts), and at present results are published only after long delays.

In 2001 until September 11 th , travel and tourism had been growing at the annual rate of 3.8 per cent and was expected to maintain that level of growth for the full year. In the event, according to WTTC estimates, travel and tourism demand worldwide in 2001 ended 1.3 per cent down on the previous year.

The real decline for the whole of 2001 as compared to the expected growth was therefore 5.1per cent, of which it has been estimated that as much as 4.4 percentage points can be attributed to September 11 th alone.

In 2002, the year-on-year decline of travel and tourism was expected to continue, with WTTC forecasting last spring a slight decrease by 0.4 per cent for the whole of 2002. The forecast was adjusted in fall when WTTC estimated a flat performance as compared to 2001. On the assumption that last year's pre-September 11th growth of 3.8 per cent would normally have continued throughout 2002, this would mean another real annual decline for tourism of close to 4 percent, of which around 3 percentage points can be attributed to the events of September 11 th alone.

The effect of the crisis on the level of revenue from international tourism in 2001 is shown in Table 2 below. The positive growth trend that prevailed throughout the 1990's was brought to an end in 2001 by a drop in the industry's income from international travellers of some 5.2 per cent at constant US Dollar prices.

Table 1

Travel and Tourism (T& T)

The Estimated Impact of the Crisis in 2001 and 2002

	2001		2002				2001- 2002
	(A) PRE 9/ 11 FORECAST	(B) ACTUAL RESULTS	(C) CRISIS IMPACT	(D) PRE 9/11 FORECAST	(E) UPDATED FORECAST	(G)= E- D CRISIS IMPACT	(H)= C+ G TOTAL CRISIS IMPACT
	Full Year Estimate 2001 Real Growth Over 2000 (Per cent)	Full Year Results 2001 Real Growth Over 2000 (Per cent)	Real Growth Loss (Per cent)	Estimate 2002 Real Growth Over 2001 (Per cent)	Full Year Estimate 2002 Real Growth Over 2001 (Per cent)	Real Growth Loss (Per cent)	Real Growth Loss (Per cent)
T& T Demand	3. 8	-1. 3	-5. 1	3. 8	-0. 0	-3. 8	-7. 4
T& T Industry Employment	2. 1	-2. 5	-4. 6	2. 3	-1. 7	-4. 0	-8. 6
	(thousands)	(thousands)	(thousands)	(thousands)	(thousands)	(thousands)	(thousands)
T& T Industry Employment	1,602.6	-1, 879.3	-3, 481.9	1,827.3	-1, 350.6	-3, 177.9	-6, 659.8

In 2001, OEF (Oxford Economic Forecasting, Ltd.) generally estimates that 85% of the variance can be attributed to the events of September 11 th (15% to independent recessionary events). In 2002, this factor decreases to 70% associated with 9/ 11 (30% to independent recessionary events).

Source: World Travel and Tourism Council (WTTC): *The Impact of Travel and Tourism on Jobs and the Economy - 2002 plus; Special Report on September 11 th Impacts*; released 17 March 2002; up dated by ILO based on: WTTC: *The Travel and Tourism Economy 2002; Special End of Year Update*, 8 November 2002.

Table 2
International Tourism Receipts

	International Tourism Receipts (billion)					Growth rate % current prices		Growth rate % constant prices	
	1990	1995	1999	2000	2001	00/99	01*/00	00/99	01*/00
US$	263.4	406.5	456.3	474.4	462.2	4.0	-2.6	0.6	-5.2
Euro	206.8	310.8	428.1	513.6	516.1	20.0	0.5	17.2	-2.1

*Based on data collected by WTO up to June 2002

Source: World Tourism Organization (WTO)

The worst losses were felt in the Middle East and the Americas, particularly North America, where international tourist arrivals were down by 6.8 per cent in the whole year 2001, but by as much as 22.6 per cent in the last four months compared to equivalent periods of the previous year.

Countries most affected by the September 11th events were the United States, with international tourist arrivals having fallen to their lowest point between September and November, on average over 30 per cent below the level of the same period the previous year. Countries in the immediate neighbourhood of the US also received significantly less tourists than at the same time the previous year, e.g.

In general, all countries that would normally have expected a high proportion of their incoming long-haul tourism to originate from the United States experienced steep declines in international tourism in the first three months following September 11. In Europe, those worthy of note include the United Kingdom (-12 %), Germany (-17%), Switzerland (-16%), Italy (-11%) and Austria (-9%) - and elsewhere, the Philippines (-25%) and Australia (-21%).

Some other countries amongst those whose tourist industries are important elements in their national economies suffered badly such as Egypt (-55%), Tunisia (-25%) and Morocco (-22%). These preliminary figures served to confirm earlier predictions that the three types of tourist destinations likely to be most affected by the events of 2001 were:

— countries highly dependent on US outbound travel;

— destinations a long distance from their main generating markets; and

— countries of the Muslim world

In addition to security aspects, the general economic downturn in 2001 also contributed to the poorer performance of international tourism in 2001 compared to the previous year. Here, the main causes are to be found in those major sending countries such as the US, Germany, and Japan. South American markets suffered from economic instability in Argentina. An additional factor for the US as a receiving country, which lost as much as 2.5 per cent on international arrivals in the first nine months of the year, was its strong currency.

Among the countries performing worse as a destination for the full year 2001, compared to the year 2000, were the US, Argentina, Brazil, the UK, Mexico, Germany, Italy, the Dominican Republic, Jamaica and the Bahamas. Other countries experienced a significant drop in their 2001 total tourist numbers year-on-year because, rightly or wrongly, they were associated with security risks, and this was for various reasons not necessarily connected to the September 11 th events.

These countries included Egypt, Nepal, and Sri Lanka. By contrast, there were some countries, notably in

Europe bordering at the East Mediterranean Sea and in Southern Europe that in 2001 continued to receive higher numbers of foreign tourists than in the previous year, probably because they provide a convenient alternative to long-haul destinations for many European tourists.

Thus Turkey, Croatia, Slovenia, Spain, Greece and Cyprus all benefited in 2001. It was also observed that several emerging tourist destinations in Europe showed strong growth in the full year 2001, notably Bulgaria, Slovakia and Estonia. France (+1.2%) also recorded some growth in 2001 versus their previous year totals, benefiting from their familiarity and proximity with European holidaymakers and even compensating a temporary 20 per cent drop immediately following September 11th which was probably due the sudden lack of Americans visiting Europe.

Australia and New Zealand reported a short period of decline in inbound tourism immediately after September 11 th , but most of these losses were partly offset by something of a boom in numbers of foreign tourists later in the year. Some countries, such as the UK, Germany, China and Canada continued to send record numbers of tourists to this part of the world throughout 2001.

They did not prevent, however, a year-on-year decline of 2.7 per cent in numbers of international arrivals, mainly accounted for by 4 th quarter decreases from Japan and the US. Notably, the region with the best performance as tourist destination in 2001 was South East Asia and the Pacific, which in spite of a decline after 11 September still ended the year with a growth of 5.5 per cent, mainly due to intra-regional tourism. Performing regions were also Africa and Central America, albeit on a small basis in absolute terms.

The United States is the country whose hotel, travel and tourism industry was most seriously affected. According to the US Office of Travel and Tourism Industries, the total number of international arrivals fell by almost 11 per cent over the whole year 2001. This was largely because of a dramatic 30 per cent drop in September, moving to a 34.0 per cent loss in October, with an average 31.8 per cent loss of business over the last four months of the year compared to the same period of the previous year. October was the worst month. The numbers of international arrivals slowly started to recover in November.

Certain countries supplying travellers to the US performed worse than others because they were more seriously affected by economic crises. These included Brazil; Germany and Japan. By the end of the year, however, it was the German market that had performed worse than any other, which is probably due to generally nervous consumer behaviour in the light of the country's poor economic performance.

Demand for accommodation in the US is estimated to have suffered a far more modest decline than international arrivals, another indication that domestic tourism was less affected and it was long-haul travel that suffered most. Accommodation demand had already declined by 6.0 per cent in the third quarter of 2001, as compared to the same period in 2000. However, the decline in the fourth quarter was markedly greater, but still only a fifth of the decline in international arrivals.

Early forecasts by the Travel Industry Association of America already suggested that after the 7.6 per cent drop in 2001, the recovery in consumer expenditure levels on travel in the US would be slow in 2002, with an annual growth rate of only 2.2 per cent. Leisure trips in March, April and May 2002, for example, were 4 per cent below the level in the same period a year ago. Overall, first quarter 2002 international arrivals to the US were down 12 per cent. Four of the top markets - the United Kingdom, Germany, the Netherlands and Switzerland - posted declines for the first quarter of 2002, but the declines are less than those recorded in the pre-September 11th months in 2001.

Mexico and Spain are the main markets posting positive growth in numbers of arrivals through the first quarter 2002, at +22 per cent and +6 per cent respectively versus the same period last year. Recovery in the US is not being enjoyed equally by all sub-sectors of the industry. Leisure tourism services are recovering faster, for example, than the sub-sector catering for business travellers.

The number of Japanese travelling abroad was down 9.1 per cent at the end of 2001 versus the previous year, according to a report released in January 2002. Whereas in May 2002 the number of bookings of foreign trips through Japan's top 50 travel agencies was still 6 per cent less than the previous year, July and August, the peak season, have been especially slow, with 10 to 20 per cent fewer bookings than in the previous year.

By contrast, the numbers of visitors to domestic destinations were up by 4.6 per cent to 2.07 million. In the period immediately following September 11 th , the largest travel agent (JTB) saw an increase of 19 per cent in their bookings for domestic tours departing during the October-December period. China experienced some impressive growth in both domestic and inbound tourism, with domestic tourism developing particularly strongly.

Total annual revenue from tourism has grown on average by 12.7 per cent over recent years, much faster than the gross domestic product (GDP) which grew by an average rate of 7.4 per cent. More than 73.34 million overseas tourists visited China during the first 10 months of 2001, an increase of 5.7 per cent on the same period of 2000, or almost double the world's average growth rate for 2001 before September 11th . The total amount spent by overseas tourists in that period grew by 9.3 per cent to US$14.8 billion.

Over two-thirds of the revenue is still, however, from domestic tourism. Spain's tourist industry, which directly employs more than a million people and accounts for 12 per cent of the economy, is suffering a protracted crisis, recording 10 per cent less visitors for the first six months of 2002 compared to the same period the previous year. The number of German visitors to Spain in July 2002 was 20 per cent lower, pushing down the hotel occupancy rate by 5.5 per cent.

Reservations made by German tour operators tumbled by as much as 37 per cent. The crisis is attributed partly to growing unemployment in Germany, but also to price increases in Spain, with German tourists preferring cheaper destinations such as Turkey and Croatia. In Switzerland, tourist numbers for the six-month winter season 2001-02 were a dramatic 6 per cent down on the previous year's winter season result. Yet this was still 1.4 per cent above the average for the previous five winter seasons.

Increased domestic tourism seems to have stepped in to replace international visitors, whose numbers dropped by 10 per cent. The number of tourists visiting from the US was nearly 20 per cent less and from Japan

31 per cent less than in the same period the year before. Overnight trips to Canada were up by 0.6 per cent for the first five months of 2002 compared to the same period in 2001, boosted by an increase in US travellers entering Canada by car.

On the other hand, the number of Canadian tourists to the US or overseas was still down by 7.2 per cent (at 1.5 million) in May 2002, which represented something of a recovery because it was down 11.3 per cent for the five months before, compared to the same period a year ago. The government of Morocco predicts that tourism revenues will have dropped by US$700 million by the end of 2002, down by one-quarter on the total revenue of US$2.7 million reached in 2001.

Morocco's tourist industry recorded a 43 per cent revenue drop in January 2002 compared to January 2001. The industry currently employs over half a million people, serving some 2.4 million foreign tourists annually. Major markets supplying most of Australia's tourists showed dramatic falls in outbound tourism during the 12 months to July 2002, with the number of visitors from neighbouring New Zealand dropping by 25.5 per cent, from the UK by 17.7 per cent and the United States by 8.4 per cent, according to the Australian Bureau of Statistics.

Overall, international visitor arrivals have fallen 8.4 per cent to 409,400 from January to July 2002, compared to the 446,900 tourists for the same period last year. These results were attributed September 11 th mainly, but Australian tourism leaders feel under pressure by the lasting downturn, leading them to reconsider their whole marketing strategy.

A return to pre-September 11th levels of international arrivals was still seen as being a long way off. After the bomb attack of October 2002, the Australian tourism industry fears negative effects of tourists avoiding Asia. Singapore and Bangkok are stopovers on the most popular route from Europe to Australia. Any disruption to the flow of tourists to them would have a severe knock-on effect on Australia. Industry reports in late October 2002, however, suggested the tourist numbers from all markets would remain largely unaffected as a result of the 12 October Bali attacks.

Employment numbers in the tourism sector do not react immediately to a decrease in business because the special characteristics of employment relationships in the sector allow for some labour cost reduction to take place before workers finally become unemployed. Flexible working arrangements such as part-time or on-call working are common for at least one quarter of the labour force and help to avoid their complete unemployment in a business crisis, albeit with reduced income.

Employees accounting for almost another quarter of the total have full time but temporary employment contracts and are the first victims of formal unemployment when reducing their working time and income becomes insufficient to address the income crisis of the enterprise. Employers usually hesitate, however, to reduce their core of trained staff. Only if a crisis persists, businesses tend to re-structure and workers are eventually laid off permanently.

The WTTC estimates a 7.4 per cent drop in tourism demand over the years 2001 and 2002 combined, instead of the 3.8 per cent growth that had been anticipated previously for each of these two years. The sector is now seen as being in a state of stagnation, which is a dramatic change in fortune considering its previously very high growth rate. The WTTC estimated that over 6 million jobs would have been lost in the tourism industry worldwide in the years 2001 and 2002, which represent 8.6 per cent of employees, or one in every 12 jobs in the industry.

The process of attempting to derive employment estimates from demand estimates has to take into account that normal growth may not result in increased employment because normal growth is achieved largely through gains in labour productivity. WTTC estimated therefore that a growth of demand by 3.8 per cent would have entailed a growth of employment by only 2 per cent. Given this proportion, the dramatic effects on employment forecasted by WTTC can be better appreciated.

WTTC foresees a modest recovery of employment in the travel and tourism industry worldwide in 2003. However, with a growth of 1.7, the year 2003 will still end with a 6.4 million jobs lost as a result of the crisis compared to the expected normal annual growth rate of 2 per cent in that year. The Travel Industry Association of America (TIA) estimates that 19 million Americans were employed directly or indirectly by the travel industry, with an annual payroll of $174 billion.

The year 2001 ended with domestic travel volumes and expenditure down 3.5 per cent and 7 per cent respectively, and volumes and expenditure from international travel to the US down 12.6 per cent and 11.2 per cent respectively. Employment in the whole industry in the USA was down 5.8 per cent for the year, with an estimated 1.1 million jobs lost. High volume tourist destinations such as Las Vegas, Orlando and Honolulu are expected to have suffered major losses in 2002 due to cutbacks in travel.

Among 315 metro areas examined by the Milken Institute at the end of 2001, many jobs would be lost as a result of the events after 11 September 2001 in New York, Los Angeles and other big cities. A ranking of industries most affected by job losses after September 11 th shows the hotel and catering sector represented by the top two categories listed. Over two-thirds of the estimated 760,000 total direct jobs expected to be lost in US metropolitan areas were in core sectors related to travel and tourism.

The general economic downturn in 2001 had already started to affect all forms of consumption and travel and tourism was probably one of the sectors that suffered most because it is a market in which consumers can easily make savings. Indeed, future variations in the level of consumer expenditure on tourism will probably be driven mainly by variations in levels of present and expected household income.

The Travel Industry Association of America (TIA) undertook three Travel Confidence Surveys in the US, one from 21 to 22 September, another from 12 to 13 October 2001 and the third from 2 to 4 November 2001. In these polls, only 14 per cent of respondents cited safety as their top travel concern. On the other hand, 42 per cent cited economic concerns as reasons for not travelling.

Nonetheless, the fear factor continued well into 2002 as a strong deterrent to travel in the US and the health of the industry continued to be affected by federal alerts, air-travel-related accidents and other concerns. A German survey of 8,000 households showed that in March 2002 only one person in ten claimed to make travel decisions on the basis of security considerations, compared to November 2001 when the proportion had been almost one person in three.

It has been predicted that tourism would recover slowly and regain the levels of before September 11 th by the third or fourth quarter of 2002. This forecast would be in line with experiences from previous security crises affecting tourism, albeit local, whose effects lasted for about one seasonal cycle.

The continuing economic slowdown in the western world, as well as more recent terrorist activities targeting tourists in Djerba, Bali and Mombasa, however, are having an added effect on the tourism crisis. The year 2002 has been one of rather little growth or even slight decline of tourism performance indicators, with the possible exceptions of the Asian Pacific region and South Africa which has recorded double digit growth of tourism out of Europe in 2002, or China which does continues to grow rapidly both as a destination and as a market.

According to German tour operators, because of higher price levels, total turnover for the 2000/01 season which ended in October grew by twice as much (+ 6.8%) as the number of bookings, reaching a total of Euro17.4 billion. For 2002, despite bookings being down, German tour operators expected a turnover close to that of 2001, mainly because certain customers are making higher value choices even if they go for shorter stays.

In general, tourism demand was in the last 12 months or so subject to important structural changes including a re-distribution of demand between countries and regions. Leisure destinations located close to important markets have prospered; domestic tourism has made a difference; long-distance international air transport has suffered more than international tourism in general due to increased short distance trips across borders; business tourism and conventions, luxury hotels, and cruises during the winter season were particularly affected, while social tourism, rural tourism, rail and road travel made gains.

Among the destinations receiving European tourists, short-haul destinations have generally benefited at the expense of long-haul destinations, with demand for North America showing the greatest fall in 2002 so far. The main long-haul destination to buck the trend has been China, but a number of other Asian destinations and South Africa have similarly recorded double-digit growth out of Europe this year.

International arrivals to countries in the European region will show little change in 2002 over last year which closed with a decrease of -0.6% in international tourist arrivals in Europe. Austria, as a typical short haul destination for European markets saw foreign leisure arrivals grow by a massive 12% in the first half of 2002. This growth, however, is expected to have eased to a rate of only around 2% for the whole year.

For France, preliminary data on international arrivals (classified hotel accommodation only) suggest that the lucrative US market remained down by no less than a fifth in the first eight months of 2002 as compared to the same period in 2001, whilst growth in the Canadian market was replaced by decline.

All international arrivals together performed at a low 0.5 per cent growth, as the performance of the major generating markets within Europe has been considerable with tourists from the UK increasing by close to 7 per cent, and arrivals from Germany still increasing by 14 per cent. The nascent trend towards short-haul, short - break holidays seems to be re-configuring the intra-regional European market, with France being perhaps the main beneficiary.

Germany as a destination lost 3.3% in the number of foreign overnight stays for the first half of 2002, according to preliminary data, which, however, was still 0.2% higher than in the same period in 2000. Most of the loss is due a decrease in long haul tourists such as from the Americas. Arrivals from within Europe suffered much less and still grew by 0.9 per cent.

Foreign travelers to Italy remarkably did not decline substantially, but expenditures did. They dropped by as much as 11 per cent in the first six months of 2002 as compared to the same period in 2001. This phenomenon is likely to exist also elsewhere, but figures on 2002 are still scarce. A slight growth of foreign arrivals to Italy is anticipated for the remainder of 2002 which will close with a growth of 0.9 per cent.

Tourist arrivals at Spain's frontiers increased in the first two quarters of 2002 by comfortable 6.9 percent, but only by 0.2 per cent in the second quarter as compared to the same periods in 2001. The summer period may not have been any better. It was, however, in the United Kingdom, where after a weak winter and spring period, July 2002 arrivals exceeded those of the year before by as high as 15 per cent and even those of July 2000. Expenditure increased less, but still by 7 per cent.

Canada had continued growing as a destination for foreign tourists during the crisis year 2001, albeit at a slower pace, since most of foreign travelers came from the USA and increasingly used surface transport, in part substituting Canada for a long haul destination elsewhere. In the first six months of 2002, however, the number of foreign tourists from the USA slightly shrunk (by 0.2 per cent), and the receiving of overseas tourism, which had been down in 2001 by 8.4 per cent (arrivals) and 4 per cent (expenditures) continued declining by 13 per cent (arrivals), reducing anticipated overall growth of foreign arrivals in 2002 to only 0.1per cent.

Japan receives one international traveler only for five Japanese outbound tourists. Out of the modest number of less than 5 million that do arrive, it is estimated that over a quarter are in Japan on business and that half of this market originates from Asia. Having suffered in 2001 only a slight 0.3 per cent decrease of the-annual growth rate for all tourism, with a higher growth rate for leisure tourists of 0.9 per cent, Japan is estimated to benefit in 2002 from an impressive growth in foreign arrivals of 16 per cent, to a large extent due to an increase of the number of tourists from China.

Outbound tourism from Japan, important for many destinations in the world, is currently forecast to record modest growth in 2002 of a maximum 1-2% after a 9% decline in 2001. The Pacific Asian countries have been doing well as destinations in spite of the world crisis in 2001 and 2002. High GDP performances in mainland China, India and South Korea suggest the trend of Asian intra-regional tourism will continue.

India as a source country appears to record strong double-digit growth in 2002, albeit on a small basis. Inbound tourism in India, however, after dropping in 2001 by a moderated 4.2 per cent (arrivals) and 5.5 percent (expenditures), continues suffering from the conflict with Pakistan and the closeness to Afghanistan. Northeast and Southeast Asia are driving the region's growth - both as destinations and as markets. During 2001, almost 65% of international visitor arrivals in Northeast Asia came from within Northeast & Southeast Asia. For destinations within Southeast Asia the proportion was over 64%. China has continued to show strong growth in 2002. In the first eight months of 2002 foreign arrivals in mainland China increased by more than 16%.

Good increases of inbound tourism have also been registered by Thailand and Vietnam. However, the impact of the Bali tragedy on the region's tourism remains to be seen. Elsewhere in the developing world, only South Africa and Central America and perhaps the Caribbean are expecting slight increases of inbound tourism in 2002 over 2001's level. The USA has been one of the source markets hardest hit by all crisis factors together: the events of 11 September 2001, the continuing threat of terrorism in 2002 and the economic recession.

A strong growth of 4 per cent or more is predicted for 2004. Such forecasts seem to have the unanimous support of the specialist community, but the risks are also clear: they depend on the absence of further terrorist attacks; more selective reactions by consumers who should not stop travelling altogether when security threats in fact are limited to a location; the development of the conflict in the Middle East and its oil price implications; and last not least on the general prospects of disposable income.

In any case, forecasts by renowned specialists and organizations seem to be highly insecure. Due to the continuing weakness of the world economy, travel and tourism demand in 2003 is likely to be substantially slower than projected earlier, with business travel in particular hit hard by the pressures on companies to cut costs and bolster their profitability.

International visitor spending is now expected to recover by a modest 1.6% in 2003 after falling 10% over the previous two years, leaving international visitor spending in 2003 more than 20% below what might have been expected if it had grown by a more typical 5% a year since 2001.

For foreign tourist arrivals to certain European countries in the years to come, forecasts indicate different growth rates. Austria will remain at a modest 2 per cent growth of foreign leisure trip arrivals in 2003. A modest turnaround, with growth of 2% to 3% is expected for the next 12 months also in Germany. In France, international arrivals are expected for 2004 to be back to the pre-2001 growth rate of over 4 per cent, albeit under the assumption that long haul tourism to France will recover.

Foreign visitors to Italy in 2003 are expected to increase by 2.7%, making a total of 39 million. Likewise, a growth rate between 2 and 5 per cent is assumed for the near future in Spain. In any event, the terrorist attack will bear on the performance of the industry in the region of South East Asia and the Pacific, the only region still experiencing strong growth in its tourism flows after September 11, 2002. Probably, the whole region will be affected, as experience shows that tourists' and tour operators' decisions and preferences reflect rather superficial perception of geographical locations and of cultural profiles of destinations.

Bali and with it the whole of Indonesia will suffer badly from the effects of the attack, whereas the impact on other countries in Asia is more difficult to anticipate, as especially East Asia and the Pacific had been experiencing strong growth in spite of the global tourism crisis of 2001. In addition, Asia's tourism, more and more relies on growing intra-regional and domestic tourism which, hopefully, will be affected less by the Bali event less than was transatlantic travel after September 11th , 2001.

Indonesia's inbound tourism had done well in the years following the economic crisis of 1997-8 which it overcame as early as 1999 in terms of tourist arrivals. Receipts from international tourism, however, remained in 1999 as much as 25 per cent short of what they were in 1996, which indicates cheaper tourist arrangements or shorter stays per arrival. In 2001, the whole region of East Asia and the Pacific was little affected by the impact on tourism of the events of 11 September: due to a high growth rate in arrivals before September 11, the region still closed the year with a growth of 5.5 per cent.

After the attack of 12 October, Bali's tourism industry virtually collapsed: Airlines cancelled and re-routed a number of their scheduled flights; tourists went home or left to other nearby destinations such as Fiji and the Philippines. As a result, hotel occupation rates tumbled from a comfortable 70 per cent to less than ten per cent. In absolute terms, it can be estimated that from an average of 100,000 tourists present in Bali at any time, not more than 15,000 stayed on.

Moreover, it can be assumed that the tourists who stayed on were of Indonesian origin as they represent 15 per cent of all visitors to Bali, and those who left were foreign tourists, leaving behind a devastated tourism economy, especially as far as foreign exchange is concerned. An estimated 5.1 million tourists visited Indonesia in 2001, contributing 5.3 billion dollars to Indonesia's balance of payments (about 9.2 % of total exports). Most of these tourists appear to end up in Bali at one stage or other.

Bali's Minister for Culture and Tourism estimates that the island's tourism economy employed a portion of 65 per cent of the total labour force, i.e. 1,1 million out of the 1.71 million people in employment in Bali with a resident population of 3 million. The hotel and restaurant sector alone produced in 2000 a share of 21 per cent of Real GDP and probably employed an even higher share of the labour force.

As Bali is considered a magnet for tourists to come to Indonesia and also visit several other parts of the country, the Minister for Culture and Tourism estimates that as many as 2.7 million people may be out of their jobs across Indonesia soon if tourism does not recover quickly. He said that Tourism employed more than seven million people in the South East Asian archipelago and last year brought in 4.7 billion dollars in revenue, or about 10 percent of Indonesia's gross national product (GNP).

Due to slower economic growth and to extra public spending to promote tourism after the Bali bomb attack, Indonesia's public finances will slide deeper into the red, by about 1.5 per cent of gross domestic product next year, up from an earlier projection of 1.3 per cent. The Indonesian economy is now forecasted to expand by just 3.5 to 4 per cent in 2003, down from an earlier estimate of 5 per cent.

Prospects to overcome the crisis are not so bad, though, if the steady high growth of international tourism to countries of the region is taken into account. Asia was the only region in the world that maintained strong, albeit uneven growth in tourism during the difficult period after its economic crisis 1997- 98. A great deal is due to the growth of intra-regional tourism in Asia.

During 2001, around 65% of international visitor arrivals in both North East Asia and South East Asia came from within the north eastern plus south eastern Asian region. Prospects of intra-regional Asian tourism count in that from China a total of seven million people traveled overseas in the first half of 2002. The main markets for Indonesian tourism, however, are still Japan and Australia, where Indonesia will make special marketing efforts to counteract the tourism break down after the Bali bombing.

Budget tourists from neighboring countries like Singapore and Malaysia, as well as many domestic visitors from Indonesia's main island of Java, are replacing tourists from Japan, Australia, and Western markets. Until the end of 2002, their presence largely prevented major layoffs in Bali's tourism industry to occur.

But the changing face of Bali tourism means the average visitor stays for a shorter time and spends much less than before-less than half, according to some estimates. Rooms were available in package tours for as little as 25 US Dollars a night. The discounts mean that the income of workers employed in Bali's tourism industry will get squeezed, even if job losses remain modest.

The terrorist attack in Bali will also have a negative impact on the outbound tourism economy of Australia and put a number of Bali travel specialists in Australia out of business. Bali and other islands in the Indonesian archipelago are popular and cheap destinations for Australian families, backpackers and surfers. According to the Australian Bureau of Statistics, in the seven months to July 2002, 144,400 Australians visited Indonesia, amounting to 7.5 percent of outbound tourists.

The Asian region may suffer from indirect effects of the bombing in Bali unnecessarily. This concern was expressed by the Association of South East Asian Nations (ASEAN) when it rejected warnings and advice issued by Western countries including the United States, Britain, Australia and Japan. Such advice had covered all of south east Asia, where tourism accounted for 10.8 percent of GDP and 8.2 percent of employment last year.

In US, national tourist authorities and tourist boards, as well as the tourism industry itself - at local and national levels - have reacted in a number of ways. One way, for example, has been to make their destinations more attractive to customers. In many cases, special committees were set up to deal with the situation after September 11th. Partnerships were established between the private sector and public authorities to tackle problems of financial bottlenecks, e.g. the funding of marketing campaigns or the prevention of bankruptcies in the sector.

The measures taken range from price reductions introduced by individual enterprises in the areas of travel, hospitality, tour operating, culture and recreation, to large-scale advertising campaigns by tourist authorities. These have often depended upon substantial injections of finance by both the industry and governments.Advertising campaigns strongly address the domestic tourism markets. For instance, a campaign run by the Travel Industry Association of America (TIA) features the slogan "See America."

A comprehensive plan of action was developed by the Travel Industry Association of America to enable the industry and government to work together to reassure the public that travel is safe while rebuilding consumer confidence in travelling both to and within the United States. The USA Small Business Association (SBA) approved a total of US$21.6 million on disaster loans for small travel agencies. The average loan size was US$50,579. One of the reasons was that SBA recognized the hardships facing travel agencies nationwide in the rapidly changing travel market, especially after September 11 th .

The SBA also recognized that travel agencies were dramatically affected by reduced airline commissions and advances in technology, specifically the use of the Internet. A campaign by the Canadian Tourism Commission (CTC) invited Canadians and near-border Americans to re-discover or discover Canada.

In fact, the Canadian Government has been supporting a massive marketing campaign by contributing the equivalent of US$13 million to help the hotel industry recover from a loss of US$3.5 billion incurred in 2001.

Austria also ran a major campaign to attract European tourists to their winter sports resorts aimed at replacing missing overseas visitors. One of the most impressive programmes to boost tourism is being developed in the United Kingdom. To overcome the country's deep crisis in international tourism, the British

Government and a number of British tourist industry organizations have announced they will back a new international campaign, boosting marketing support for the British tourist industry to the tune of £ 40 million. The government will provide up to £20 million for this new initiative addressed to seven main market countries and aiming to recover at least half of the estimated £2 billion.- 35 - lost by the tourism industry last year. The campaign features over 1,000 special offers put together by both big and small companies throughout the industry, giving discounts of sometimes as much as 50 per cent.

The New Zealand government announced that it is to make US$2.5 million available for the expansion of New Zealand's official tourism classification and quality-grading company, Qualmark, in order to help attract more tourists through improved quality of services.

Another example of government support is that of India where, among other relief measures implemented, a 10 per cent expenditure tax on all food and beverages served by hotels was lifted in federal budget announcements in the spring if this year.

In Japan, the government is providing financial support to the troubled travel industry, of which 99 per cent consists of small and medium-sized enterprises. The government's credit association is doubling the maximum loan guarantee for tourism enterprises and government-affiliated financial institutions are doubling the ceiling for unsecured loans.

In general, the tourism sector has been given increased attention by public authorities as a result of the 2001-2002 crisis. Even in southern Europe, which did comparatively well immediately after the September 11 th

, both State authorities and the public were sensitized by the crisis and initiatives for private-public partnership increased. One example is a special Euro-Mediterranean group that has been set up on the initiative of Spain and Tunisia to encourage tourism cooperation between the countries of the European Union and Northern Africa.

Ranking of most frequent cost reduction measures in the U.S. lodging industry after the events of September 11th In a number of countries, some measures as described above have already been taken. Others will need more time to develop. The ILO has monitored the developments in the industry with particular emphasis on human resources development, because it was recognized that information on the employment effect of the crisis is still scarce.

There is also a need to find more examples of positive action taken by enterprises, social partners and governments aimed at mitigating the impact of the crisis on employment and working conditions. Furthermore, improved methods of measuring the impact on employment of developments in tourism, as well as a series of case studies on good practices, will help to strengthen the capacity of the tourism sector to handle human resources challenges both in normal times and in times of crisis.

In cooperation with different partners, the ILO is prepared to assist developing countries in the modernization of their training systems in the tourism sector in order to help reduce their vulnerability to increased international competition. Raising the quality of services is one possible way of helping to rebuild tourists' confidence after a crisis and it might also have a chance of increasing customer loyalty to a particular destination.

These reactions can have a significant effect on a country's revenue from tourism in a very short period of time. The ILO is developing a Tourism Labour Accounts System which is a methodology to measure employment and working conditions in the tourism sector. It will help interested member states to collect and analyse relevant labour data on a continuous basis and in connection with the Tourism Satellite Accounts whose methodology was approved by the United Nations Statistical Commission in 2000.

In view of the disastrous impact of the terrorist attacks of September 11 th , the International Labour Organization (ILO) convened a meeting in October 2001, with an informal framework involving representatives of governments and Employers' and Workers' organizations in the hotel, catering and tourism sector from different member States. There were also representatives present from Workers' and Employers' organizations acting at the international level.

The meeting reviewed the impact of the events and the social partners formulated their recommendations on how the crisis might be overcome quickly, and how the impact of other events affecting the tourism sector in the future might be limited. The ILO constituents made a number of recommendations addressed to Governments, such as:

— Recognize to a still greater degree the critical role that the hotel and tourism sector plays in the economy and afford it an appropriate place in national strategic economic planning.

— Organize widely supported campaigns and projects to promote tourism in general.

— Develop additional tourism strategies, including strategies relating to domestic and intraregional tourism, to moderate the negative effects of the cyclical nature of tourism.

— Adopt policies aimed at increasing the number of people for whom tourism opportunities are available, including special provisions to encourage those on lower incomes to engage in tourist activities.

— Encourage consultation amongst the social partners at national and local levels in the hotel and tourism sector to mitigate the negative effects of the crisis and promote tourism in general.

Employment and Globalisation in Tourism Sector

When the ILO Governing Body created the ILO Industrial Committee for the Hotel, Restaurant and Tourism Sector, which subsequently became the Committee for the Hotel, Catering and Tourism Sector, the sector included:

(a) hotels, boarding houses, motels, tourist camps, holiday centres;

(b) restaurants, bars, cafeterias, snack bars, pubs, night clubs, and other similar establishments;

(c) establishments for the provision of meals and refreshments within the framework of industrial and institutional catering (for hospitals, factory and office canteens, schools, aircraft, ships, etc.);

(d) travel agencies and tourist guides, tourism information offices;

(e) conference and exhibition centres.

Industrial Classification of all Economic Activities (ISIC), the latest edition of which is ISIC Rev. 3. In that classification, the sectors most relevant for the ILO definition of the sector are Hotels and restaurants and Activities of travel agencies and tour operators, Tourist assistance activities. Other organizations concerned with tourism, including governments, intergovernmental organizations and NGOs, often use much broader definitions of the term than that used by the ILO. They subsume under it all services and products consumed by tourists, including transport.

In the ILO denomination of the sector, the part referring to "tourism" only covers travel agencies and tour operators. Hotels and catering, including restaurants, are considered by most organizations to belong to the "tourism characteristic industries" and therefore subsumed under tourism, although in some countries only a small part of their services is for tourists.

However, the fact that the ILO definition of the sector thus differs considerably from the concept of tourism used by other organizations does not prevent most concerns about the development of tourism from being shared by those organizations. One such concern is the sector's potential to provide employment. Nevertheless, the ILO's focus on labour issues is unique as it includes all working and employment conditions in the HCT sector.

As an economic concept, tourism is defined in "demand side" terms, as it comprises all services and goods consumed by tourists as well as all investments made to satisfy that consumption. A tourist has been defined by the United Nations as a traveller or visitor. The credibility and international comparability of "tourism statistics" depend heavily on:

(1) a consensus regarding the choice of "tourism characteristic industries", i.e. those industries on which tourism demand has the most important direct impact, and an estimation of the "tourism ratio" of their output; as well as

(2) the methods used to calculate the indirect effects on the output of many other industries.

Statistical presentations differ in whether they include such indirect or induced effects in the measurement of tourism in the economy. Probably the most inclusive choice of industries is the one adopted by the World Travel and Tourism Council (WTTC), a private organization. It takes into account industries whose "tourism ratio" is low but whose products and services represent high value, such as the construction and operation of transport infrastructure.

The demand side nature of tourism is the basis of a methodology for Tourism Satellite Accounts (TSAs) developed by the World Tourism Organization and OECD and adopted by the United Nations Statistical Commission early in 2000. The ILO has been cooperating with those organizations in accordance with the mandate given to it by the Tripartite Meeting on the Effects of New Technologies on Employment and Working Conditions in the Hotel, Catering and Tourism Sector in 1997, with a view to providing a methodology for the production and presentation of tourism-relevant labour statistics to supplement the TSAs.

A proposal has been formulated by the ILO for a tourism labour accounting system (TLAS) within that framework, based on its work on a general labour accounting system. A detailed "employment module" presenting labour-related issues was already attached to the TSA by the OECD, but this module does not provide the necessary framework for linking the different units, variables and classifications used when collecting labour statistics from many different sources. Some early efforts towards TSA presentations have already been made by a number of pioneer OECD countries on the basis of figures from national accounts systems as required in the methodology adopted by the United Nations Statistical Commission in 2000.

The World Travel and Tourism Council (WTTC) has been producing Tourism Satellite Accounts using a simulation method and based on a non-systematic variety of statistical sources. The contribution of tourism activities to national GDPs, direct and indirect, varies by country and region as illustrated by the WTTC's estimates.

The Caribbean is the most tourism oriented region in the world. It is estimated that in 2000, tourism employed 3.1 million people either directly or indirectly, thus accounting for 13.4 per cent of total employment. Direct employment in the tourism characteristic industries alone amounts to 5 per cent of total employment.

Visitor expenditures contributed an estimated US$17 billion, or 18.4 per cent, to export revenues. Countries whose international tourism receipts exceed 5 per cent of GDP or 10 per cent of export revenues are considered to be "tourism countries" for the purposes of the World Trade Organization.

Tourism is expanding in almost all countries including the developing countries. In fact, mass tourism involving domestic and regional travel is becoming an important phenomenon in several developing countries of Asia, Latin America, the Middle East and Africa, where the proportion of the population actively participating in domestic and regional tourism is predicted to grow considerably. In particular, regional tourism originating from China is expected to change the Asian tourism industry profoundly within the next one to two decades.

Employment in Hotels

Employment in hotels and restaurants is presented in table 1. The table shows data supplied to the ILO by a limited number of countries using the International Standard Industrial Classification of all Economic Activities, Revision 3 (1990), which allows a distinction to be drawn between hotels and restaurants and commerce in general. What is striking about the information given in table 1 is the high proportion of unpaid labour in the hotel and restaurant trade in some countries, including the industrialized countries.

This reflects a large number of small entrepreneurs and their non-remunerated family members. In some countries, this proportion is increasing as paid employment is growing more slowly than total employment, although in general growth rates for both are high. Tourism across national borders represents a variable but generally large proportion of total tourism. Especially in a number of developing countries a significant proportion of gross domestic product is generated by activities designed to satisfy international tourism, which thus represents an important export activity in many countries.

Globally, the World Tourism Organization (WTO) predicts that the number of international tourists will reach almost 1.6.billion by the year 2020, and that international tourism receipts will exceed US$2,000 billion. The estimated growth of world international tourism arrivals of 4.5 per cent per annum will pose enormous challenges and opportunities for those regions and countries seeking to benefit from tourism while avoiding its negative impacts.

As shown in table 3, the world's top ten tourism destinations are France, Spain, United States, Italy, China, United Kingdom, Canada, Mexico, Poland and the Russian Federation. France welcomed 73 million visitors in 1999, followed by Spain with almost 52 million and the United States with 48.5 million. The top ten tourism destinations in the world in terms of tourism receipts are the United States, Spain, France, Italy, United Kingdom, Germany, China, Austria, Canada and Greece.

The United States earns the most from tourism, with total tourism revenues of US$74.4 billion in 1999, followed by Spain and France. Even though tourism is a global industry, the majority of receipts still accrue to the Americas and Europe, reflecting both the fact that closeness to origin of the travellers still matters and the fact that countries in these regions have had the time, resources and demand needed to develop their tourism industries.

For many countries, international tourism is an indispensable source of foreign currency earnings. According to the World Tourism Organization, tourism is one of the top five export categories for 83 per cent of countries and the main source of foreign currency for at least 38 per cent of them.

Table 3. World's top 15 receiving countries for international tourism: Arrivals

Country	1998 (million)	International tourist arrivals 1999 (million)	Market share 1999 (%)
France	70.0	73.0	11.0
Spain	47.4	51.8	7.8
United States	46.4	48.5	7.3
Italy	34.9	36.1	5.4
China	25.1	27.0	4.1
United Kingdom	25.7	25.7	3.9
Canada	18.9	19.6	2.9
Mexico	19.8	19.2	2.9
Russian Federation	15.8	18.5	2.8
Poland	18.8	18.0	2.7
Austria	17.4	17.5	2.6
Germany	16.5	17.1	2.6
Czech Republic	16.3	16.0	2.4
Hungary	15.0	12.9	1.9
Greece	10.9	12.0	1.8

Source: World Tourism Organization (WTO): *Tourism highlights 2000*, 2nd edition, Aug. 2000 (1999 preliminary data).

In 1998, international tourism and international fare receipts (receipts related to passenger transport of residents of other countries) accounted for roughly 8 per cent of total export earnings from goods and services worldwide. Total international tourism receipts, including those generated by international fares, amounted to an estimated US$532 billion, surpassing all other international trade categories.

As a by-product of the rapid fall in the real costs of long-distance travel, the developing regions of the world participate fully in the worldwide growth of international tourism. However, market shares vary strongly from one county to another and within very short periods, reflecting the economic or security crises affecting different countries or regions.

Tables 4 show the growth rates in receipts from international tourism in the different regions of the world as defined by the World Tourism Organization and their respective market shares.

Table 4. International tourism receipts by region: Market shares (%)

	1985	1990	1995	1997	1998
World	100.0	100.0	100.0	100.0	100.0
Africa	2.2	2.0	2.0	2.1	2.2
Americas	28.2	26.2	24.8	26.6	26.8
East Asia/Pacific	11.2	14.9	18.4	17.2	15.4
Europe	53.8	54.4	52.2	51.1	52.7
Middle East	3.5	1.7	1.9	2.1	1.9
South Asia	1.2	0.8	0.9	0.9	1.0

Source: World Tourism Organization (WTO): *Tourism highlights 2000*, op. cit.

Changing Face of tourism industry

Mass tourism in and from the industrialized countries is a product of the late 1960s and early 1970s. Since then a number of interrelated developments in the world economy, such as overall economic growth and various other socio-economic changes, government policies, technological revolution, changes in production processes and new management practices, have converted part of the industry from mass tourism to so-called "new tourism".

The latter connotes the idea of responsible, green, soft, alternative and sustainable tourism, and basically refers to the diversification of the tourism industry and its development in targeted, niche markets. Competition in the new tourism is increasingly based on diversification, market segmentation and diagonal integration. The identification and exploitation of niche markets has also proven to be a great source of revenue within new tourism, suggesting that further diversification and customization can be expected in the years to come.

Market segmentation - as exemplified by ecotourism, cultural tourism, cruise and adventure tourism - is clearly in evidence and is experiencing great success. New niche markets are constantly being identified in an attempt to diversify the industry further. Customization has also begun to play an important role in the industry.

Tourism players are attempting to gain a competitive edge by catering for the individual needs of clients. The tourism product has thus been transformed over time from being completely dominated by mass tourism to an industry that is quite diversified and caters more to the individual needs of its participants.

Today, new consumers are influencing the pace and direction of underlying changes in the industry. The "new tourists" are more experienced travellers. Changes in consumer behaviour and values provide the fundamental driving force for the new tourism. The increased travel experience, flexibility and independent nature of the new tourists are generating demand for better quality, more value for money and greater flexibility in the travel experience.

The new consumers also reflect demographic changes - the population is ageing, household size is decreasing and households have greater disposable income. Changing lifestyles of the new tourists are creating demand for more targeted and customized holidays. A number of lifestyle segments - families, single parent households, "empty nesters" (i.e. couples whose children have left home), double-income couples without children - will become prevalent in tourism, signalling the advent of a much more differentiated approach to tourism marketing.

Changing values are also generating demand for more environmentally conscious and nature-oriented holidays. Suppliers will therefore have to pay more attention to the way people think, feel and behave than they have done hitherto. In recent years the niche market has become an important factor in the tourism industry reflecting the need to diversify and customize the industry and ensure the sustainability of the product.

The main niche markets (sports travel, spas and health care, adventure and nature tourism, cultural tourism, theme parks, cruise ships, religious travel and others) hold great potential and are developing rapidly. The growth of the cruise tourism sector is an interesting case in point. Between 1980 and 1999, the cruise industry grew at an average annual rate of 7.9 per cent.

The Caribbean is the most important geographic market for the cruise industry, accounting for over half of all cruises taken in 1996. Since 1984, cruise visitor arrivals have increased every year except 1987 and 1989. In addition, between 1996 and 2000, the growth rate for cruise arrivals is expected to far exceed that of stay-over arrivals.

The rapid growth and development of the cruise tourism industry opens key opportunities but also poses a number of threats to their Caribbean destinations. The environmental and economic impacts of cruise tourism are increasingly the subject of discussion. Moreover, given the pace and magnitude of its development, the cruise industry is directly competing with land-based tourism and, as a result, poses a growing threat to hotels and other land-based resorts and businesses in the Caribbean.

Rise of cultural tourism and ecotourism

The rise of these forms of tourism, in which indigenous peoples also play a role, reflects an interest in other environments, ways of life and cultures. Moreover, it reflects a desire on the part of the tourist for more socially responsible types of tourism, underscoring the idea that some profits should be returned to indigenous peoples in the form of income, and in keeping with environmental concerns.

Ecotourism is a fruitful source of jobs and, if provided with the appropriate means, can provide lasting employment in regions not reached by other industries. Local inhabitants can be employed as guides and rangers, in the lodges or hotels created to deal with the influx of tourists, or as interpreters. Labour is required to build and maintain the infrastructure needed to open up access to the regions in question.

The economic benefits to remote communities, if carefully managed and shared fairly among the local people, can be used sensitively to raise educational and living standards without obliterating local culture. Local populations also have great expertise in the conservation of their own surroundings and may therefore be well employed as experts on the safeguarding of the biodiversity in their regions. Research suggests that ecotourism is growing substantially.

In Africa, safari tours have existed for many years, but over time negative effects have become apparent, and a more careful approach has been adopted in certain cases. An example is Kenya, where the Masai people were evicted from their traditional lands in 1984 to make way for conservation and safari tourism. As a result, the Masai began poaching and killing the wild animals, in the belief that this would stop tourists coming and they would get their lands back.

Subsidiary employment effects include jobs in transportation and building and as hotel and catering staff in the many safari lodges in the area. The profits realized by this system are used for the maintenance of boreholes, animal husbandry and education for the Masai. Tourism can thus be seen to work for the local population, both in terms of providing job opportunities and in raising education and training levels.

One of the challenges presented by ecotourism is not just the creation of employment in remote areas, but the offer of higher quality opportunities for indigenous people. In Brazil, local people were initially employed in lower paid, less visible positions in hotels and lodges, since they had little notion of how to deal with tourists. Subsequently, the Brazilian Ministry of Labour, with funds from FAT (the Worker Assistance Fund), established the National Professional Tourism Education Programme.

Over the past three years the programme has been used to provide a large body of professionals in various tourism-related activities and is expected to lead to greater numbers of local people being engaged in employment in national parks and reserves. Similarly, in Uganda, the Budongo Forest Ecotourism Project (BFEP) was started in 1993 with the specific intention of invol·ing the local population in forest conservation.

Activities such as biking, horse riding, trekking, rafting and kayaking, as well as relatively high-risk and more recent sports such as canyoning, are becoming increasingly popular. The Adventure Travel Society, based in Colorado, estimates that the industry expanded by 38 per cent between 1991 and 1997, generating US$220 billion through sales of adventure travel and associated equipment. A number of vocational training institutions - for example, the Nelson Polytechnic in Wellington, New Zealand - are offering courses in adventure tourism, which shows the rising popularity of the field and points to possibilities for employment as accompaniers, monitors and guides.

In India also, the Karnataka State Tourism Development Corporation (KTDC) has decided to set up three adventure sports/tourism academies to provide two-year courses to train skilled adventure tourism personnel. The KTDC operates three adventure tour camps near Bangalore and has difficulty finding staff to operate the camps. The training institutions are to be run by private sector partners and adventure tourism companies, but the KTDC plans to arrange tour operator sponsorships for the students, linked to employment following completion of their courses.

The globalization of agriculture markets has placed a strain on certain domestic markets, at the same time as agreements within the World Trade Organization have reduced subsidies to producers and liberalized trade. Farmers in traditionally agrarian areas of Europe have had to seek alternative means of supplementing their income. This may partly explain the rise of rural and nature tourism.

In the United Kingdom, it is estimated that 90 per cent of all farms provide some form of tourist accommodation, while the figures also show that 25 per cent of European holidays are taken in rural, as opposed to coastal, areas. The break-up of farming collectives in countries in transition to a market economy has also encouraged the spread of rural tourism establishments.

The sector remains largely unstructured. It is characterized by large numbers of owner-operators who expand their activities to include the provision of board and lodging. While it may stabilize a precarious financial situation for a population whose income has fallen, its effect in terms of job creation is doubtful. This is not to underestimate its popularity: in 1997, the French public spent a total of 315 million nights in rural vacation areas in France.

In India, the Karnataka State Tourism Development Corporation has introduced a "bed and breakfast" concept in Coorg and Chikmagalur near Bangalore, where there are very few hotels but many large private residences where house owners could provide paying-guest accommodation. The scheme has proved successful and is to be extended to other parts of the State. The professional part of the sector appears keen to safeguard itself from what might constitute unfair competition, since the type of rural establishments described do not have to meet the same standards as fully fledged hotels.

Taxation in catering and tourism sector

The industry is in favour of ongoing tourism investment and accepts the need for effective taxation. However, large increases in tax on international tourism and travel, which is basically an indirect tax on export earnings, cannot be implemented without an impact on levels of business, and consequently on employment. The globalization of the economy and the ease with which we can now move about the world will only serve to highlight this, as comparative costs of different destinations become apparent through ICT.

The WTTC is of the opinion that industry growth, investment and job creation is most likely to occur in destinations with supportive tax regimes. The European Union allows a lower rate of value added tax (VAT) on accommodation and certain other tourism and leisure facilities. Ireland chose to lower VAT on accommodation and restaurants in the 1980s, and it is estimated that this led to the creation of 30,000 jobs in the industry.

The WTO argues that reductions of this sort, by improving international competitiveness, can also result in higher total tax receipts, rather than the opposite. Within the European Union, the situation regarding taxation is highly complex, with different rates of VAT and other taxes applying in different countries, and different rates applied within countries depending on the sectors.

Travel agencies offering packages will clearly link up with hotels charging lower taxes. The industry therefore sees a need for reductions in taxes that are perceived to be damaging productivity, and for harmonization of taxation levels, not only within the European Union, but at international level.

Role of SMEs in employment

The last two decades have seen a growing recognition of

the important role of small and medium-sized enterprises (SMEs) in employment creation and the promotion of economic growth and development. The general characteristics, potential and problems of SMEs have been a subject of debate within the ILO for many years.

SMEs form the majority of enterprises throughout the world in general and in the tourism and hospitality industry in particular. The characteristics of SMEs in the tourism industry include flexibility, direct control of service delivery, personalized and tailor-made service, entrepreneurial activity, strong local character, willingness to cater for special interest groups, employment of family members, flexible timetables and multiskilled personnel.

SMEs play an important role in the European hotel and catering sector. The average number of employees per enterprise ranges from 3.3 to 7.5, except in the United Kingdom, where it can be up to ten. SMEs, because of their fragmented nature, lack opportunities to make economies of scale. They are often operated by non-professionals who lack the marketing skills required to optimize their business opportunities, and they experience difficulties in gaining access to training.

The Tourism Conference held from 20 to 22 May 1998 in Llandudno under the United Kingdom's Presidency of the European Union, proposed a ten-point framework for action in support of SMEs in tourism. These recommendations were aimed, among other things, at modernizing the sector in the light of globalization by raising awareness among SMEs of business support systems, information technology and the possibilities open to them in respect of finance, and by providing affordable possibilities for better training for managers/owners and staff.

The European Union High Level Group on Tourism and Employment has called for a Community initiative which "promotes the development of innovative tourist businesses by young entrepreneurs". Large hotel chains are able to establish their own training programmes, often by linking up with public or private education and training establishments. Governments may also provide assistance to SMEs unable to upgrade their employees' skills themselves.

One example from the United Kingdom is the Tourism Opportunities Programme (TOPS), which was set up to provide public sector subsidized training. The scheme provides affordable training in areas where individual hotels could not justify creating specialist courses, and may thus benefit from economies of scale.

Large hotel groups such as Accor and Radisson have their own central reservation systems (CRSs) which the public can access via the Internet. While a degree of interactive reservation may come to the SME sector, especially in view of the potential marketing possibilities provided by the World Wide Web, SMEs are for the time being largely dependent on traditional distribution channels. Through their tourist offices, many governments provide networking and marketing services for their hotels and tourist establishments at national or regional level, either free of charge or at a reasonable cost.

In France and Spain, tourist offices in larger towns and cities are able to give information about availabilities in establishments within the regions they cover. In the United Kingdom, in the London districts of Greenwich and Islington, the visitor and tourist information centres provide information not only regarding the larger hotels, but also on bed and breakfast establishments in their areas. These centres provide an important support mechanism and marketing tool for very small businesses, which might otherwise remain marginal. The problem of how to classify the levels of service provided in such establishments is another area in which governments could act.

Finance is a recurring problem for small enterprises. The entrepreneurs concerned may have no professional background or training, and this naturally deters banks. Their financing requirements tend to be small, with consequently higher transaction costs for banks, and such businesses also have a problem finding guaranteed collateral.

Many governments intervene by providing interest rate subsidies or guarantees to lending institutions, and some governments, as in India, Indonesia, the Republic of Korea, Malaysia, Pakistan and the Philippines, have imposed minimum quotas on financial institutions for loans to SMEs. According to ILO estimates, the informal sector worldwide employs about 500 million workers. With the process of globalization, the informal sector is gaining importance as a result of its job creation capacity.

Since the industry is a labour-intensive sector, the high labour costs may be one reason for recourse to undeclared work in some areas, and employers have criticized governments for failing to integrate informal sector activities into the formal sector. Hotels and restaurants, by providing entry-level employment, play a role in bringing workers from the informal sector into a more formalized labour market, and employers argue that lower labour costs would increase this effect.

The situation of some particularly vulnerable groups of workers is a key issue in view of the technological changes occurring in the hotel and tourism industry. The ILO's World Employment Report 1998-99, which deals with national policies in a global context, stressed the need for equity in reform programmes to ensure that vulnerable groups benefit from the processes of globalization in general and from new economic opportunities created by market reforms in particular.

Tourism employment is an alternative to traditional and more rigorous work, such as agriculture or fishing, and provides both men and women with greater occupational choices. Young people who are marginalized are generally poor, with little education and training.

Migration also tends to exacerbate the process of marginalization. Eighty-five per cent of young people live in developing countries, and that proportion is expected to increase to about 89 per cent by 2020. UNESCO estimates that approximately 96 million young women and 57 million young men are illiterate, the majority in developing countries.

According to more recent estimates, the proportion of women in the tourism industry (excluding the informal sector) has risen to 46 per cent, while in catering and accommodation they represent over 90 per cent of all employees. They occupy the lower levels of the occupational structure in the tourism labour market, with few career development opportunities and low levels of remuneration.

The greater incidence of unemployment among women is attributed to their low skill levels and their low social status in many poor countries. They also tend to be the first affected when labour retrenchment occurs as a result of recession or adjustment to new technology. It should also be noted that the majority of workers in subcontracted, temporary, casual or part-time employment are women.

Child Labour in Tourism Industry

Child labour is a matter of grave concern, robbing children of their childhood, stunting their growth and hindering the development of their countries. An estimated 13-19 million children and young people below 18 years of age (10-15 per cent of all employees in tourism) are employed in the industry worldwide. However, these figures take no account of the number of children working in the informal sector in ancillary activities. Other estimates also suggest the extent and scale of the phenomenon in the industry.

Child labour in tourism is common in both developing and in developed countries. Many boys and girls below 12 years of age are engaged in small business activities related to hotels and restaurants, the entertainment sector or the souvenir trade, often as porters or street or beach vendors. They are frequently subjected to harsh working and employment conditions. 2 million children throughout the world are subjected to commercial sexual exploitation and thus exposed to such concomitant risks as HIV infection.

Tourism must bear its share of responsibility for this trade. There are many factors which can drive families and children away from their homes towards poles of tourist attraction in city centres or coastal regions. Those factors include:

— civil or national conflicts;

— ethnic rivalries;

— family breakdown;

— excessive urbanization which aggravates overcrowding and creates a range of social ills;

— diminishing agricultural resources; and

— other severe economic hardships, such as rising unemployment, national financial crises, and cutbacks in subsidies or other measures introduced under structural adjustment programmes.

Child refugees from Somalia and Rwanda are exploited in a number of ways on the beaches of Mombasa. Active recruitment and trafficking agents are a factor in all this, but the lure of consumerism and its images cannot be ignored. These are all underlying reasons which help to explain why children and young people are driven into exploitative employment in the tourism industry, or, worse still, in the sex trade, which operates very lucratively in the tourist centres of Asia, Africa, Latin America, the Caribbean, and the transition countries.

The sexual exploitation of children of both sexes, as practised through child prostitution and child pornography, forms a sometimes hidden part of the overall commercial sex sector. Although a worldwide phenomenon, it is more prevalent in Asia than elsewhere. In the Philippines, frequently quoted estimates of the number of children involved range from 30,000 to 60,000; a very recent report quotes the figure of 75,000.

The United Nations has defined child sex tourism as "tourism organized with the primary purpose of facilitating the effecting of a commercial sexual relationship with a child". Certain holiday destinations are now frequented by paedophiles. At national level, pimps, taxi drivers, tour operators (by organizing package sex tours), hotel staff, brothel owners and entertainment establishments all work together to satisfy foreign tourists' demand for prostitutes.

At the international level, agents disseminate information about particular resorts where such practices are commonplace. Increasing concern over the appalling conditions of child labour have led to the adoption of new international instruments and action plans by the international community. In 1999, the International Labour Conference unanimously adopted the Worst Forms of Child Labour Convention, and Recommendation No. 190.

These instruments declare "the use, procuring or offering of a child for prostitution, for the production of pornography or for pornographic performances" to be one of the worst forms of child labour, and urge ILO member States to take immediate and effective action to prohibit and eliminate it as a matter of priority. The pace of ratification of Convention No. 182 is the fastest in ILO history, with 41 ratifications in just over 16 months.

The quest for improved child protection can also be measured by the worldwide concern about child labour that has been expressed in a number of international forums. Among these are: the Stockholm World Congress against Commercial Sexual Exploitation of Children, 1996; the European Meeting on the International Dimension of Sexual Exploitation of Children, held in

Madrid, 1998; the European Meeting of the Main Partners in the Fight against Child Sex Tourism, held in Brussels, 1998; and the UNESCO Expert Meeting on Sexual Abuse of Children, Child Pornography and Paedophilia on the Internet, held in Paris in January 1999.

The Global Report on the international dimensions of sexual exploitation of children, which is a follow-up of the Stockholm World Congress, includes recommendations which cover a wide range of measures to protect children from sexual exploitation and ensure that their abusers are properly prosecuted and convicted anywhere in the world.

UNICEF has presented a study on extraterritorial criminal laws against child sexual exploitation which includes a series of recommendations on ways of stopping the international market for sex tourists and paedophiles who travel to other countries to exploit children sexually.

The Stockholm World Congress is scheduled to be followed by the second of its type in December 2001 in Yokohama, Japan. With regard to specific action-oriented initiatives originating from the tourism industry itself, IH&RA participates in a task force against child sex tourism coordinated by the World Tourism Organization along with other trade association partners such as the Universal Federation of Travel Agents' Associations (UFTAA), the International Air Transport Association (IATA) and non-governmental organizations such as ECPAT (End Child Prostitution, Pornography and Trafficking).

The Youth Career Development Programme launched jointly by the Singapore-based Pan-Pacific Hotels and Resorts Group and UNICEF in 1995 is another commendable initiative. This 20-week programme sets as its objective the provision of basic skills in the hospitality industry and long-term social and economic security for young girls exposed to the risk of commercial sexual exploitation.

Trade unions have also undertaken action against child sex tourism. The IUF has drawn up a model collective agreement aimed at preventing child sex tourism for use by its affiliated organizations in the tourism industry.

Migrants in Tourism labour market

The impact of international migrant flows on the tourism labour market of receiving countries is another important issue, whether it concerns daily commuters, seasonal workers or permanent migrants. The majority of them are drawn into lower paid, informal or casual employment in services. Although many migrant workers stay for a number of years, they often remain at low skill levels compared to local workers.

In Austria between 1970 and 1995, there was a marked increase in migrant labour employed in hotels and restaurants as compared to other sectors of the economy, but stricter immigration laws in the mid-1990s led to a reduction of new entries. In 1996, the percentage of foreign workers in hotels and restaurants was 51.2 per cent in Switzerland and 30.9 per cent in Germany. In Spain, the coastal resorts employ a large number of illegal immigrants.

A comparative study of hotel employment and employee development in Finland, Spain, the United

Kingdom and Bulgaria suggests that increasingly global tourism markets and the more permeable national and labour market boundaries resulting from economic, political and social integration in Europe have led to a growth in numbers of transient workers and increasingly elastic labour market migration - mainly inwards to the United Kingdom and Finland, and mainly outwards from Spain and Bulgaria.

In Canada, the labour force in the accommodation sector has historically come from marginalized segments of the labour market, including immigrants. In the hotel sector, there has been a gradual shift towards the employment of newer immigrant groups. In Germany, McDonalds employs a large number of immigrants, mainly from the former Eastern Bloc, and others who are disadvantaged on the labour market owing to language problems and lack of recognition for previous qualifications.

In Denmark, the participation of immigrants in the tourism labour market is increasing markedly. From 1980 to 1995, the proportion of immigrants in the tourism workforce increased from 4.9 per cent to 7.6 per cent. More than 12 per cent of all foreigners active in the Danish labour market are employees or business owners in the hotel and restaurant sector, and in 1995, 16.7 per cent of immigrants active in tourism were running their own enterprise.

Danish employees in tourism enjoy relatively better employment conditions than their immigrant counterparts, who have lower job status, lower earnings, and more family responsibilities. Danish workers in part-time employment are predominantly women, whereas the foreigners are mostly men.

The hotel, restaurant and catering sector remains an area in which use is frequently made of undeclared labour. In some countries, this may involve the clandestine employment of illegal foreigners who are willing to accept less advantageous conditions of employment than nationals. It may also take the form of employees being declared as working for a certain limited number of hours while actually working longer hours and receiving supplementary payments in cash, thus enabling both employer and employee to avoid payment of a proportion of social insurance contributions. Undeclared labour is employed mainly in small enterprises where cash is available outside the official accounts.

2

Technological Directions in Tourism

On the demand side, consumer preferences for flexible travel and leisure services provide a strong impetus for new tourism. On the supply side, technology plays an important complementary role in engineering new tourism. The applications of technology to the travel and tourism industry allow producers to supply new and flexible services that are cost-competitive with conventional mass, standardized and rigidly packaged options.

Technology gives suppliers the flexibility to react to market demands and the capacity to integrate diagonally with other suppliers to provide new combinations of services and improve cost effectiveness. In the travel and tourism industry a whole range of interrelated computer and communication technologies is being introduced.

The system of information technologies (SIT) comprises computerized reservation systems, teleconferencing, video text, videos, video brochures, computers, management information systems, airline electronic information systems, electronic funds transfer systems, digital telephone networks, smart cards, satellite printers, and mobile communications. Each technology component identified in the SIT - for example, computers - can be and usually is fully integrated with the other components.

For example, computer-to-computer communications allow hotels to integrate their front offices, back offices and food and beverage operations. This internal management system for hotels can in turn be fully integrated with a digital telephone network, and they then together provide the basis for linkage with hotel reservation systems which can be accessed by travel agents through their computerized reservations terminals (CRTs).

Computerized reservations systems have emerged as the dominant technology among others being diffused throughout the travel and tourism industry. In the United States, travel agents are using satellite printers at corporate offices to issue tickets directly at the point of demand. Interactive automated ticket machines (ATMs) have also been introduced.

These consist of a computer with an attached printer that enables passengers to research schedules and fares, make reservations, purchase tickets and obtain boarding passes without the intervention of a human agent.

The Internet is a global network connecting millions of computers. As of 1999, the number of Internet users was above 200 million worldwide, and that number is growing rapidly, involving more than 100 countries. It is estimated that there were 63 million World Wide Web users in Europe in 1999. The United Kingdom, with almost 13 million Internet users, currently registers the highest number of users among the European countries.

Use of the Internet for travel booking and planning is increasing rapidly. The rapid diffusion of information technologies throughout the travel and tourism industry is expected to improve the efficiency of production and the quality of services provided to consumers, and to generate increasing demand for new services.

Impact of Globalization

The driving forces of globalization impacting upon travel, hospitality and tourism. The air transport industry, which is located mainly in the industrialized regions and in the newly industrialized countries, is a key determinant in the development of tourism. It is expanding twice as fast as the general output of the world economy, with further growth potential expected over the next two decades. In the developing countries, air transport accounts for nearly 80 per cent of international tourist arrivals.

In 1998, the industry provided 28 million jobs worldwide, and by 2010 the number of people travelling by air could exceed 2.3 billion each year, with over 31 million jobs provided. Today, liberalization of air transport largely means market access for private carriers and cabotage rights. The liberalization of air transport, traditionally pursued at the bilateral level, is now being carried to the level of multilateral trade agreements.

The recent trend towards the liberalization of air transport notably through the proliferation of open skies agreements, has thus raised the issue of air transport liberalization as a discipline to be debated in the framework of the General Agreement on Trade in Services (GATS). Multi-bilateral negotiations are already under way on an open skies agreement between the European Union and the United States.

If they succeed, 70 per cent of the world's international air traffic will be covered by the agreement. It is expected in that case that the agreement will serve as a model for other international air services agreements. The formation of international alliances is an important development in the field of aviation. Airline alliances have become widespread and are still evolving, with partnership relationships becoming more intertwined and complex.

The major airlines in the Americas and Europe are the most active in securing alliance agreements. The main motivation behind such alliances is the need to minimize costs while maintaining the quality of global services and extending connections throughout the world.

Alliances can take various forms including: cooperative arrangements; wide-ranging strategic alliances, most notably the so-called "mega-alliances"; groupings and concentrations at national level, as in the case of the United States; purchase or franchising of small regional companies by major operators to carry their customers to hub airports; and regional civil aviation markets. Other trends which characterize the changes under way in the context of airline liberalization include:

— partial or full privatization and restructuring of government-owned airlines;

— partial foreign ownership of airlines;

— equity investment in foreign carriers;

— updating of airline alliances by cancelling outdated or non-performing agreements;

— airline consolidations at the national level;
— joint ventures, either between airline companies or between airline companies and equipment manufacturers or independent maintenance companies; and
— outsourcing with no provision of maintenance service.

Effects of liberalization

Recent privatization initiatives have ended the protection of national airlines by governments in a number of developing countries. However, the possibility of the market becoming dominated by a single private company is perceived as a serious risk. In some cases, developing countries that have liberalized their air transport sectors as part of a policy to promote tourism have found themselves dominated by one or two foreign airlines.

Some bankruptcies and closures have taken place in countries where distressed national airlines were not or could not be rescued by governments. In this context, a review of the GATS annex on air transport services is intended to draw international attention to the need to design a system that enables developing countries to compete effectively in the world market for air transport.

With regard to the liberalization of air transport as a whole, the trend is increasingly for each State to choose its own pace of change, using bilateral, regional or multilateral mechanisms. In developed countries there has been a clear tightening of competition policies to prohibit governments from providing subsidies. It is well known that many bilateral agreements have resulted in inefficiency as they were based on market access restrictions, price control and protection of money-losing carriers.

Full liberalization of air services as implemented in 1997 in Europe boosted the development of "low-cost" services and their integration in the European aviation scene. Although these services still account for a rather small share of the passenger market, their marketing impact is increasingly being felt throughout the industry. It is estimated that around 25 per cent of passengers on United States domestic services use "low-cost" airlines, as compared to approximately 5 per cent in Europe.

Another result of liberalization is that new route opportunities have opened up, stimulating new demands without tampering with major carriers' shares and therefore creating new opportunities for fare reductions. Some major European flag carriers have already created their own "low-cost" airline subsidiaries. The low-cost market as it stands has considerable growth potential.

Europe's low-cost airlines are finding plenty of untapped markets. Both Ryanair and easyJet have placed orders for significant numbers of additional aircraft to almost double their capacity over the next four years to meet this new demand. The challenge for low-cost carriers is to strike the right balance between maintaining low costs, low prices and high aircraft utilization and establishing a presence at a certain minimum number of airports.

A further development of the concept of the low-cost airline sector has been the advent of "seat-only" sales on charter airline flights, rather than as part of a package holiday. This has resulted, for example, in the formation of the European Leisure Group (ELG), an alliance of European charter and scheduled airlines.

The General Agreement on Trade in Services (GATS) became part of the "New World Trade Order" under the aegis of the World Trade Organization as established by the Uruguay Round in 1994. The functioning of GATS is based on the interplay of fundamental standards in commercial law, procedural regulations for their implementation and specific commitments in which member States document sector-specific limitations or concessions.

GATS has universal coverage and includes a comprehensive definition of trade in services comprising four "modes of supply". They are: cross-border movement of services; movement of consumers; commercial presence; and the presence of natural persons, and to these modes the three principles of liberalization enshrined in GATS. GATS thus provides a framework for the progressive liberalization of trade in services through commitments made by the World Trade Organization member countries concerning the abovementioned principles and their applications to one or more modes of supply.

Future negotiations under GATS will provide an opportunity for developing countries to address trade barriers to their services. The tourism sector had already undergone various forms of liberalization before the Uruguay Round. It is also considered to be one of the service sectors most liberalized through sector-specific commitments made by signatory States.

The number of commitments by the World Trade Organization members made so far in tourism under the

GATS is rated as the highest of all sectors. Of 127 GATS signatory States, only eight have not made commitments in tourism and travel-related services. In the hotels and restaurants subsector, which offers the greatest potential for far-reaching liberalization within tourism, it is mostly low and lower-middle- income economies in Africa and Latin America that have liberalized market access for foreign investors in the "commercial presence" mode: 64 per cent of all signatory States belonging to the group of LIEs and 75 per cent of LMIEs, but only about half of the group of high-income economies (HIEs) have "no restrictions" to that mode.

On the other hand, it is not surprising that "presence of natural persons" is the least liberalized mode of supply: in 117 of the 119 countries signing commitments in travel and tourism-related services, there are restrictions on the movement of hotel staff. Sixty-eight countries refer to their non-sector-specific commitments which mostly offer only temporary stay for business visitors, intra-corporate transferees and professionals.

Only an ancillary service to tourism (airline computer reservation services), is included in an annex on air transport services. Possible impact of GATS on air traffic services, tourism services production, free movement of people, market access and labour markets. Most air traffic services are not covered by the Agreement's disciplines. The main organizations responsible for air transport are now examining ways in which the GATS could contribute to future air transport liberalization.

The GATS provides a framework for negotiating temporary entry of service personnel into the territory of other parties. The movement of natural persons is a necessary condition for developing countries' participation in the world market for services. Developing countries have given priority to making commitments under the GATS relating to the movement of natural persons, partly taking into account their competitive labour cost advantage.

The World Tourism Organization, for example, is developing a range of quality standards to be applied at tourism destinations. Recognition of diplomas and professional qualifications is another precondition for the movement of natural persons abroad. This calls for the harmonization of diplomas and mutual recognition agreements between countries.

Several countries have notified mutual recognition agreements under GATS Article VII.4. It is hoped that the GATS will increase the recognition of qualifications across borders. Considerations within the framework of the GATS may also become relevant for the migration to the richer countries of persons who overstay their tourism visas and take up work. Many of them work in hotels or restaurants where in some countries they form a significant proportion of the labour force.

The increased scale and diversity of global communications systems and their declining costs, which are rapidly narrowing telecommunications gaps, have helped to make international migration easier. With regard to the movement of consumers, tourism is an example of the services sector where consumption abroad is particularly relevant. Nevertheless, the movement of tourists is in some instances constrained by the difficulties associated with the delivery of visas, hard currency regulations and insufficient availability or inadequacy of air transport services to and from tourist-receiving countries.

Specific commitments made under the GATS to encourage greater participation by developing countries in world services trade relate to three main areas:

— first, the strengthening of the domestic services capabilities of developing countries through access to technology on a commercial basis, which is normally achieved through the employment and training of local personnel in foreign-owned hotels;

— secondly, improving the access of developing countries to distribution channels and information networks.

In the tourism sector, this means access to computerized information and reservation networks managed and owned by entities in the industrialized countries; thirdly, the liberalization of market access in sectors and modes of supply of export interest to them. According to GATS Article XIX, developing countries can attach additional conditions to such access aimed at achieving the development objectives of Article IV, namely the strengthening of their domestic services capacity and improvement of their access to distribution channels and information networks.

The liberalization of services is likely to have both positive and negative impacts on the labour force in relation to wages and employment. Increased competition by better equipped hotel and restaurant companies from abroad may in the short term lead to job losses in local enterprises. However, foreign firms will employ local people, increasing local employment and contributing to a higher standard of living.

The world economy is currently witnessing two distinct trends - globalization and regionalization - and within this context States as well as companies are pursuing a variety of different strategies in order to become more competitive. Shifting patterns of production and consumption across the world are also reflected in the rise of new international tourism destinations, particularly in the East Asia and Pacific region.

This has given rise to increasing regional, intra-regional and interregional competition and to new challenges in terms of investment needs and human resources development, especially with regard to training and labour mobility. The impact of trade blocs on the hotel, tourism and catering sector can be gauged by the strategies adopted to create an environment conducive to tourism development.

The European Union has launched a wide range of initiatives and activities through a variety of programmes in such broad areas as sustainable development, dissemination of information, training and enterprise promotion. The main thrust of social policy in the European Union is the improvement of labour market conditions with a special focus on those excluded from the labour market and the unemployed.

European Union labour laws and social policy are having a positive impact on the tourism sector. Of importance here is the Maastricht Social Protocol which has benefited seasonal and part-time workers and small businesses. Other policies that have proved beneficial to the development of tourism include the free movement of workers across Europe, harmonization of qualifications and tax incentives for education and training.

The North American Free Trade Agreement (NAFTA) benefits the travel and tourism industry in many ways. It promotes demand for direct air and charter/tour bus travel in the region, guarantees that tourism companies will receive national treatment in all three countries and maintains high quality of tourism services by encouraging the expansion of telecommunications links between the United States and Mexico.

MERCOSUR is, in economic terms, the world's fourth largest trade bloc, covering a population of 205 million people. Economic integration, through the practice of free trade with no tariff or pre-tariff restrictions between the member States of the bloc, has led to increasing cross-border flows of labour, goods and investment.

MERCOSUR's concern is to tackle labour relations, employment and social security issues and the short-term negative effects of integration on labour in the member States. Tourism development is a priority on the agenda of the Association of South-East Asian Nations (ASEAN). Its development strategy incorporates:

— promotion of sustainable tourism development;

— preservation of cultural and environmental resources;

— provision of transportation and other infrastructure;

— simplification of immigration procedures; and

— human resources development.

A plan of action on ASEAN cooperation in tourism shows the emphasis that is being placed on investment in human resources development, with a special focus on tourism education and training with a view to upgrading the skills needed to meet the demand for improved service quality and professionalism in the tourism and travel industry and thereby sustain ASEAN's overall competitive advantage.

Cooperation in tourism education and training is being intensified through the sharing of resources, skills and training facilities provided by tourism training institutions through technical assistance and experts.

Computerised Reservation System

Computerized reservation systems (CRSs) have been developed by large air carriers since the 1970s to process flight reservations, but have evolved and expanded over time to provide other air transport-related services. Each airline has its own CRS and they are interconnected through global distribution systems (GDSs).

A huge number of Internet on-line reservation systems act as a kind of virtual agent, most of them having direct links to one or several CRS/GDS. The CRS and GDS systems have become the main distribution and marketing tool in the international tourism trade and have greatly enhanced the efficiency of travel agents' business operations. They cater to the needs of different market segments, including management of air and land transport services, the hospitality sector and entertainment services, as well as other ancillary services which make commercial transactions and risk coverage feasible. As a result, they have become increasingly important and are extensively used by all suppliers of tourism services.

There is some concern that developing countries' suppliers may well be left out because GDSs can present major barriers to entry owing to their unfavourable access conditions. A number of African and south Asian countries are poorly represented in these systems because of structural handicaps such as the low level of tourism development in general and their underdeveloped hospitality sector. The poor representation of small service suppliers in GDSs adversely affects the dissemination of information on their tourism products, thereby holding back their sale and marketing of tourism services.

This leaves such suppliers, especially SMEs, at a competitive disadvantage compared with those who are represented in the major GDSs. GDSs in many developing countries, particularly in Africa, are established in the form of joint ventures with local partners - for example, the national carrier - but operate within a de facto monopoly. This leads to excessive user fees and hinders their potential for developing tourism.

Travel agents in developing countries are at a disadvantage with regard to the use of modern technology compared with their counterparts in developed countries because of poor information network infrastructure and the shortage of professionals to manage, operate and maintain the system. Human resources assume importance in the operation of GDSs and other electronic media, and this calls for staff training in mastering the systems and their application to marketing, through specific training programmes provided by both the public and private sectors.

Use of Internet for marketing

Deregulation, globalization and radical shifts in leisure

and tourism behaviour on the demand side have driven the tourism industry towards information-oriented activities, as seen in the introduction of IT systems in a wide range of spheres in the tourism and leisure sector. The increasing use of the Internet for destination marketing, direct sales and bookings has given rise to electronic tourism markets and at present tourism is among the most important application domains in the World Wide Web.

The development of websites has made possible the direct delivery of comprehensive travel information about tourism suppliers to potential travellers. Text-based websites with photos and graphics linked to websites of tourism suppliers at the destination is another innovative approach to marketing.

Developing an effective travel website has now assumed importance for obvious reasons. International tourists are increasingly using the travel websites on the Internet that were launched by most international companies in the late 1990s. On-line sales in Europe, for example, represented only 0. 1 per cent of the European travel market, and in 1999 only 1 per cent of the world's airline tickets, hotel and other bookings were purchased over the Internet, although the proportion of airline and other ticket sales through the Internet is expected to grow sharply over the next three to four years.

The Internet helps to make travel products globally accessible at much lower cost—without transaction costs and the costs of intermediaries—and has comparatively low entrance barriers with regard to financial resources and human know-how. For many suppliers, tourism marketing efforts are increasingly focusing on Internet users. A new business environment and new ways of doing business have sprung up as a result of the accessibility and relatively low cost of the Internet which is bringing businesses and consumers, buyers and suppliers on-line.

Internet and Internet protocol technology is the driving force behind the growth of e-business. The Internet will have repercussions on business in the areas of e-commerce, e-working and e-procurement. A recent global survey of more than 500 business leaders lends support to the idea that e-business will be a key factor in competitive advantage in the future. In the sphere of air travel, attempts are frequently made to bypass traditional travel agencies by direct booking via the Internet or corporate implant offices.

Customer demands are becoming more technology driven, such as the demand for professional travel and billing management in place of mere ticket issuing. Advances in technology in the hotels and tourism industry, as exemplified by readily available information to guests and employees, faster service delivery, shorter cycle times and more dynamic markets, also require prompt action from service suppliers if marketing opportunities are not to be lost.

Strategies of growth and concentration through mergers and acquisitions are becoming increasingly important from the mediators' perspective as a response to cost and performance pressures in international business travel. In addition, traditional kick-back contracts are increasingly being replaced with new performance-oriented arrangements. All aspects of business are being reshaped by the Internet and its related technologies, intranets and extranets.

Hospitality enterprises will need to focus on providing customers with real-time access to rates and product information. The Internet also provides hotels and restaurants with opportunities to redesign the way in which they interface with employees and suppliers. The high growth in global commerce accompanied by the emergence of electronic commerce driven mainly by the Internet has raised concerns about the need to regulate cyberspace by setting standards to regulate the use of the Internet for all aspects of travel and other fast-growing categories of electronic commerce.

The primacy of the rules of the network economy will significantly lower transaction and communication costs, thus allowing more flexible pricing. The regulation of the Internet through the enactment and implementation of cyber-laws and privacy standards will most probably be perceived as an encouraging initiative which will guarantee safety and security in Internet business transactions, especially in shopping and travel accommodation bookings, where the Internet is most frequently used.

Hoteliers and restaurateurs have already expressed marked interest in these technologies as means of exploiting the advantages which can be derived from, for example, increased guest loyalty and market share. By using data warehousing and data mining as well as the Internet, the hotel industry can provide higher levels of personalized services and value. The Internet is turning out to be the most sought after amenity in hotel rooms, providing communications access, information, entertainment and education.

It enables more self-service oriented transactions to take place, especially in the area of reservations booking.

Information technology impacts on all aspects of the hotel organization value chain and transcends all departmental and geographical boundaries. Decisions on technology-related issues need to be made at top management levels of companies, and this means that qualified information technology personnel are needed at those levels.

Another key issue is the source of investment capital required to fund information technology initiatives. Lack of capital seriously hinders the implementation of information technology and competition for fund sourcing. The Internet has brought about some very significant technological changes that enhance its capabilities and viability and its potential to drive electronic commerce.

Besides introducing new and innovative business models in both the business-to-business and business-to-consumer markets, the Internet has shortened the value chain and put pressure on all players, especially intermediaries, by giving rise to the so-called "disintermediation" process, that is, the elimination of intermediary organizations such as travel agencies and global distribution systems (GDSs).

These intermediary organizations are gradually being replaced by new emerging intermediaries. On-line service and ticketless travel have significantly reduced the need for travel intermediaries, as a result of which travel agents in the United States, for example, have seen a reduction in commissions paid to them by airlines.

The use of information technology in the tourism industry is determined by such factors as the scale and complexity of tourism demand and the degree of expansion and sophistication of new tourism products.

Tourism plays an important role in a significant number of developing countries, many of which enjoy a competitive advantage.

There are more opportunities in the field of e-commerce than in any other existing technology which developing countries can exploit to their advantage in order to improve the marketing of their tourism products. However, in the developing countries, tourism development is constrained by a number of factors which have been summarized by UNCTAD.

Computer software represents one of the largest segments of services delivered through the cross-border mode of supply, with a growing number of developing countries using the Internet both to market and to deliver these services.

In Indian software industry, electronic commerce facilitates access to new markets, as well as being cost saving and time saving. However, its effectiveness depends to a large extent on the establishment of a sound telecommunications infrastructure; in most low-income countries, that infrastructure is inadequate. A wide range of factors prevent the great majority of developing countries from accessing foreign markets through the Internet.

Those factors include monopoly pricing for long-distance telephony, uncertainty about the regulatory environment, lack of human resources, lack of awareness among developing country companies of the relevance of the digital economy, and the high cost of setting up, upgrading and redesigning a significant e-commerce site. The status of the developing countries' readiness for e-commerce is an important issue.

Providers of tourism services must also have the capacity to invest in or have access to the physical infrastructure for logistics services and information technologies. The major obstacle to increased use of e-commerce in developing countries is the lack of pervasive low-cost telecommunications, broadcasting, Internet services and associated infrastructures, especially in rural areas.

At the same time there is a need to involve more hotel and tourism enterprises from developing countries in the actual use of information technologies and information networks. If African businesses fare better than consumers in terms of accessing e-commerce, they nevertheless face the same infrastructure problems, although progress has been made in the development of e-commerce activities.

The shortage of IT specialists on the market, especially in the developing countries, is a serious impediment, given the rapid growth in Internet use. The demand for IT skills is increasing and the need for retraining of existing employees in both the public and private sectors in hotels, tourism and catering is clearly felt.

One solution would be for developing countries to take advantage of forthcoming GATS negotiations to ensure access for their suppliers to the most important generating markets, and they could make use of certain mechanisms provided for in the GATS which might enhance the contribution of trade in services to development. They could also seek commitments with respect to the training of personnel and access to the distribution channels which are essential to tourism exports, as provided for in Articles IV and XIX of the Agreement.

Since the mid-1990s, multinational hotel companies entering foreign markets have devised a wide range of management strategies or methods in response to competitive challenge such as the rapid development of information technology, sophisticated demands from well-informed and knowledgeable travellers and the rise of electronic business-to-business market-places and to seize the opportunities opened up by the network economy.

Within each company, core competencies are being developed and renewed through rapid information technology development, international expansion and market cooperation, relationship management, development of customer-oriented products and services, structural re-engineering, new marketing initiatives and campaigns, and quality control.

Within the context of international expansion and market cooperation, companies have had recourse to a number of competitive methods which merit attention. The growing number of alliances is changing industry structures and the level of competition has shifted from the individual company level to alliance groups level. The last five years have witnessed nine major mergers and acquisition transactions in the international hotel market-place.

There are other goals and objectives which strategic alliances can fulfil in order to assist multinational hotel firms in strengthening their market positions, improving partnership relations and supplying diversified products and quality services to their customers. These goals and objectives include:

— acquisition of new information and communication technology;

— distribution of products and cross-marketing between food-service providers and hotels;

— distribution and cross-promotion of bank credit cards and financial services between banks and hotels;

— consolidation of transportation and hotel services;

— co-promotion of hotels and films and media.

Some well established international companies provide their expertise by leasing out management teams to run local firms. The contracting company benefits from the knowledge and experience of the international company and from its reputation for quality and good service.

With the evolution of the hotel industry towards a more consumer-oriented service, it is the brand rather than the company which assumes importance. In the United Kingdom hotel industry, for example, branding has become very topical and operators are increasingly recognizing the value of brands in delivering profits. The brand is thus turning out to be a fundamental element in defining the market, so much so that it is the name of the brand under which a hotel trades that carries weight, rather than its ownership and management structure.

Vertical integration is another strategy that plays a dominant role in particular segments of the tourism industry. For a long time, tour operators have been establishing backward and forward linkages in the areas of service production. Their backward integration includes hotels and charter airlines. These operators also control all stages of distribution via far-reaching forward integration of retail distributors and travel agencies, marketing and package tours sales.

This is also true of airlines which extend their level of integration far into the field of primary tourism and travel-related services via their charter airlines which have interests in tour operators, retailers and travel agencies. By contrast, hotels and hotel chains hardly pursue vertical integration strategies at all.

An expansionist strategy of diagonal integration is geared to the provision of the broadest possible array of tourism-related service markets by a company, with a view to cutting costs, making the most of synergies between individual markets and achieving systems gains. This includes, for example, the joint use of computerized reservation systems by carriers and travel agencies under the umbrella of a holding company or cooperation between credit card suppliers and tour operators or travel agencies offering the special insurance services of a holding partner.

In the accommodation industry, an impressive amount of consolidation took place in the 1980s, bringing more and more hotel brands under fewer and larger corporate umbrellas. Consolidation offers certain advantages such as cost reduction in the areas of reservation systems, loyalty programmes and staff training and other fixed costs associated with hotel management.

One pertinent issue frequently referred to by the developing countries is the need to reduce the risk of "leakage" of foreign exchange earnings. The developing countries in particular are usually unable to make the most of the economic and development potential of tourism, firstly, because of the high import content of construction materials and equipment and consumable goods needed to cater to the needs of international tourism and, secondly, because of the repatriation of income and profits earned by expatriates. The latter is in fact a major obstacle to tourism development.

Nevertheless, a number of advantages can be derived from international companies in terms of capital investment and know-how and technology, management and marketing expertise, training and consultancy. This enables countries lacking the skills base and expertise needed at all professional levels to run, develop and operate tourist establishments for an international clientele to benefit from the transfer of expertise and technology.

In a globalized economy, skills become an important determinant in competitiveness. The changing composition of the workforce and work patterns resulting from globalization processes in the industry have brought about new challenges in human resources development. Training policies in the hotel, tourism and catering sector will need to be reviewed in a new climate of empowerment and retention of staff. This is particularly the case in many parts of the world where there is an acute shortage of qualified staff to fill positions created by an expanding industry.

An internationally focused human resources policy calls for a change in personnel policies and strategies which implies, among other things, management commitment to transnational strategies, the development of IT skills and procedures to support transnational operations in a number of ways such as knowledge and information transfer, and an awareness of the different national policies on health and safety, occupational standards, dismissal, discrimination and workers' rights.

Impact of SMEs

Globalization has brought about a range of opportunities

and challenges which have put additional pressures on SMEs. In addition to having to cope with the effects of globalization, they need to adapt to new business conditions in terms of product positioning and product development facilitated by information technology, with all its potential benefits in terms of market access for SMEs.

The potential of SMEs for achieving economies of scale is very limited and the use of computer reservation systems (CRSs) has not spread significantly, quite apart from the fact that SMEs are already disadvantaged because of their high average unit production costs. SMEs are forced by market conditions to install new systems and train their staff to use tourism-related technology but find it difficult to invest in training or staff development, mainly because of limited investment resources and the fact that many SMEs in the hotel, tourism and catering sector are managed by a generation of staff have had no formal training in the sector.

In a globalized market, SMEs need to pursue new survival strategies. The tourism sector at the destination has to cope with the increasing problem of seasonality encountered by many coastal resorts. Competitive advantage then depends on organizational competencies and capabilities. Local SMEs have to face a number of conditions imposed by large overseas companies. Large tour operators strongly influence the way in which hotels operate at their featured destinations and the prices that they charge, particularly in mass market beach resorts and in short season resorts (e.g. ski resorts); they may also impose conditions on local suppliers, such as compliance with environmental protection standards.

In developing countries, SMEs play an important role in employment creation but are hampered by low productivity levels, poor product quality and lack of access to credit and training. The impact of capital outflows from developing countries resulting from e-commerce is another issue which needs attention. The need to develop competition policy-related disciplines in this area is also clearly felt, in view of the need to establish safeguards to prevent abuse by dominant suppliers.

Such issues arising from e-commerce might be addressed in future GATS negotiations. The global hotel market encompasses a wide range of types of accommodation full-service hotels, bed and breakfast inns, suites, self-catering short-term apartments and time-share properties. Distribution and intermediation are increasingly recognized as factors critical to the competitiveness and success of the tourism industry in general and of small and medium-sized tourism enterprises in particular.

The latter need to develop effective distribution channels either to meet the needs of their independent clientele or to provide direct booking mechanisms to reduce their dependency on tour operators. Hospitality organizations and hotel chains already rely on customer bookings through the Internet.

The challenge for tourism sector SMEs is to be able to compete for their market shares and take advantage of emerging opportunities and associated benefits to enhance their profitability and viability in the global market-place. Cost and benefits for developing Internet presence for small and medium-sized tourism enterprises:

— Costs of purchasing hardware, software and communication package

— Training cost of users

— Design and construction of Internet presence

— Cost of hosting the site on a reliable server

— Ongoing maintenance and regular updating

— Marketing the Internet service and registration of domains

— Development of procedures for dealing with Internet presence

— Commissions for purchases on-line by intermediaries

— Advertising fees for representation in search engines and other sites

— Interconnectivity with travel intermediaries such as TravelWeb, ITN, Expedia

Benefits

— Direct bookings, often intermediaries and commission free

— Global distribution of multimedia information and promotional material

— Low cost of providing and distributing timely updates of information

— Global presence on the Internet, 24 hours a day, 365 days a year

— Durability of promotion

- Reduction of promotional cost and reduction of brochure waste
- Great degree of attention by visitors to website
- Reduction of time required for transactions and ability to offer last minute promotions
- Low marginal cost of providing information to additional users
- Support of marketing intelligence and product design functions
- Development of targeted mailing lists through people who actively request information
- Great interactivity with prospective customers
- Niche marketing to prospective consumers who request to receive information
- Interactivity with local partners and provision of added value products at destinations
- Ability to generate a community feel for current users and prospective customers

SMEs in the tourism sector are constrained by the growing concentration and globalization of tourism supply. In addition, lack of professionalism and inadequate management and marketing skills, the absence of economies of scale and limited access to the necessary capital, human resources, marketing expertise and technology, over-reliance on a limited number of distribution partners and inadequate formal education or business training are among other deficiencies which put them at a competitive disadvantage.

Overall, the inability to market their products adequately seriously affects their profitability and ability to survive in the globalized economy. SMEs are highly reliant on existing distribution channels, namely, intermediaries such as tour operators, travel agencies, travel information centres and tourist guides. It can be argued that the gradual reduction of SMEs' reliance on intermediaries will enable them to become more profitable, flexible and adaptable and to produce customized tourism products in order to satisfy niche markets.

This will also require a rethink of all strategic and operational practices with regard to SME development, as well as development of entrepreneurs' managerial skills and professionalism, training in marketing and management and on the use of information technology. SMEs can benefit in a number of ways by applying information technology to develop their product, thereby enhancing their market position and increasing their profit margins.

Information technology offers new management and business opportunities and can be applied strategically to gain competitive advantage, improve productivity and performance, facilitate new ways of managing and organizing, and develop new businesses. Although information technology entails risks and costs, its underutilization could increase the vulnerability of SMEs and aggravate any competitive disadvantage as greater use is made of IT systems, including CRSs, GDSs and the Internet, to locate and purchase tourism and accommodation products.

With regard to electronic data interchange (EDI), for example, empirical evidence suggests that EDI is perceived by SMEs as too complex and cumbersome and that the initial investment is too high. Although SMEs play a major role in the international tourism and hotel industry, their vulnerability becomes quite obvious in the highly demanding business environment characterized by competition generated by globalization and the transformation of tourism demand.

Globalization of the industry means that SMEs in the tourism sector compete in a multinational environment where only organizations capable of providing exceptional value or cost advantage will survive. The opportunity of achieving economies of scale in distribution channels, reservations, marketing, advertising, administration, personnel management, technology adaptation, new product development, training and bulk purchasing of raw material and equipment, has been instrumental in the creation of major hotel chains, international consortia, management contracts and multinational franchising companies, and has placed the independent operator at a disadvantage.

The overall trend in the hotel industry appears to be towards a gradual but steady switch from independently owned and operated hotels to hotel chains. SMEs seem to be the weakest and most vulnerable members of the industry and will need to seek competitive advantages if they are to compete and maintain their market share in an increasingly globalized economy.

Worldwide, employment within the tourism economy is estimated at 192.2 million jobs. By 2010, this should grow to 251.6 million jobs. This includes employment created by fixed capital formation activities and by providers to the tourism industry. Direct employment for tourist consumption amounts to about 3 per cent of total employment worldwide. In some countries, however, the proportion is three times higher.

The industry is heavily dominated by SMEs: in Europe, for example, there are 2.7 million SMEs operating in the sector, representing almost all HCT enterprises. Some 94 per cent of this segment are micro-enterprises employing fewer than ten people. SMEs employ over half the labour force working in the industry.

Although tourism is a growth industry and a major creator of value added, the industry is vulnerable to a variety of economic, ecological, geopolitical and meteorological factors, and over-reliance on it can be dangerous for a country. Economic recession and the impact of natural disasters or terrorist attacks can devastate the sector in a country for several years.

One example is the recent Asian financial crisis which resulted in a substantial tourism downturn throughout 1997 and 1998 in affected countries, which have only recently started to recover. Another is the war in the Balkans, which has seriously reduced tourism income in that area. Events of this kind represent the extremes of a recurrent uncertainty in an industry which is characterized by the seasonal nature of many of its activities and by important fluctuations even during normal periods.

These factors shape the structure of the tourism labour force, making it difficult to maintain high permanent staffing levels. There is a generic tendency to operate on the basis of a core staff and to employ the labour needed for day-to-day operations under atypical contractual arrangements.

As the ultimate "just in time" deliverer of goods and services, the restaurant sector has to face exceptional peaks of work as, to a lesser degree, does the hotel sector - either during holiday periods or, for example, to deal with congresses. The industry responds by maintaining a large pool of temporary labour on which it can draw in response to demand. These workers are likely to be young and/or female.

The necessary availability is often found among students wishing to combine university or vocational studies with flexible working hours in hotels and restaurants. The industry employs mostly young people, and indeed for many of them provides the point of entry into the world of work. Women may also find flexible arrangements convenient as a means of balancing family obligations and work.

In the same country, 14.5 per cent of workers in the industry were under 20 years old; - in the Netherlands, the average age of workers in the industry is 23 years; in Denmark, 50 per cent of all employees are under 30 years old; in Spain, over 50 per cent of all employees are under 34 years old, and the 16-24 years age group represents 20.4 per cent of total employment in the sector; - some 58 per cent of workers in the hospitality sector in Australia are women; in Denmark, the industry is 62 per cent female; in Italy there is a 50 per cent split between men and women; in the Netherlands 52 per cent of employees are women; and, although in Spain the figure is 42.5 per cent, the number of women employed in the sector is increasing.

In an industry which employs a large proportion of young, mobile people, turnover is bound to be high, and recruitment is a habitual problem in the sector for this and other reasons. However, one hotel in the United Kingdom has introduced a customer host scheme, under which older recruits - with a minimum age of 55, but generally over 60 - are recruited to help out as concierges during peak periods. Such employees often have considerable experience in the industry and may have a lower absentee rate.

Role of ICTs

Information and communications technology (ICT) systems which integrate the power of the Internet, customer relationship management and supply chain management in a seamless, one-source destination site, allow a variety of operations - product selection, ordering, fulfilment, tracking, payment and reporting - to be performed with one easy-to-use tool. By cutting out one or more layers of the purchasing structure, these systems yield cost savings by putting the buyer in some instances into direct contact with the producer.

They also have employment implications, as intermediaries find that their share of the market is shrinking, with inevitable reductions in labour requirements upstream of the HCT sector. Technology which facilitates on-line hotel, restaurant and theatre reservations or travel arrangements will have an impact in terms of staff reductions on the front-desk hotel staff who used to perform those functions. This technology also calls for a different range of skills from employees.

Although systems designers, aware of the rapid turnover among front-desk staff, are working on products that are easier to operate and thus reduce training time for new recruits, the technology is changing so fast that knowledge becomes obsolete ever more quickly. Training will therefore become a continuous need and the remaining jobs will require greater skills.

Many hotels are examining the possibility of installing personal computers in their guest rooms, and some have indeed already done so. This allows customers to use hotel rooms as their offices. Increasing numbers of business guests are also travelling with their own portable computers. Hyatt International Hotels are an example of how new job profiles may be created as a result of this technology. The group has introduced "technology concierges" in their deluxe properties worldwide.

These specialist employees, known within the group as "compcierges", are trained to help guests to set up their mobile communications equipment, to explain how to use the in-room technology, hook up laptop computers, provide support in accessing e-mail or the Internet, and so on. They may also help to locate local retailers that service computers and stock software.

While technological expertise is essential, the emphasis is on service; all the team members come from a hospitality background and have in addition received the training needed to become electronic troubleshooters. ICT equipment installed in hotels also requires maintenance and planning departments, making this a new field with job creation potential, although such work may largely be subcontracted to outside operators.

Swissôtel has established an ICT department employing ten people, which is now an independent, profitable element of the company. The Carlson Hospitality Group also has a knowledge technologies division, which was created to ensure the smooth operation of the reservation and customer information systems installed in the group's 600 hotels throughout the world.

The new technology is also being used by a number of companies as a means of raising skills levels. Domino's Pizza has developed interactive, learner-centred programmes to guide young employees through the steps involved in making a pizza. Computer-based coaches will soon be available to guide employees through all stages of customer relations. Companies will invest in these new techniques to fulfil their training needs.

Hotel managements are studying technologies which will reduce the attention which guests require from hotel staff. These include: electronic key cards which will open doors and act as credit cards for all on-site purchases; management systems which record the time guests are likely to check out, so that room service may be programmed more efficiently; and cleaning staff equipped with hand-held computers, linked to the hotel's property management system (PMS), so that information can be centralized and constantly updated in real time.

The Canadian Regional Office of the Hotel Employees and Restaurant Employees International Union (HEREIU) has expressed concern that such systems will allow hotel companies to computerize almost all everyday front-office operations. Where customers can make their own reservations via the Internet, they could replace switchboard operators altogether. HEREIU further maintains that new in-room technologies such as video check-out systems will replace front-line workers, while electronic keys will be able to tell the PMS exactly how long each employee has spent cleaning a room, and may thus tend to promote an aggressive productivity policy.

The International Union of Food, Agricultural, Hotel, Restaurant, Catering, Tobacco and Allied Workers'

Associations (IUF) notes that placing the emphasis on time-saving and labour-saving technologies also means that the pace of work is faster, and argues that in reality, "labour-saving" and "time-saving" are inclined to mean reductions in the numbers of workers. In the IUF's view, the ultimate consequence of time-and-attendance computer software, which provides information on guest arrivals and departures so that workers can be dispatched to their duties immediately, is the dehumanization of work.

New technologies will also result in structural changes in restaurant kitchens. Use of the "sous-vide" technique, where food that has been totally or partially pre-prepared or pre-cooked is supplied directly to the restaurant, means that a large number of cooking operations can now be outsourced to independent suppliers or to centralized, chain-based kitchens.

New methods of food preservation, such as freezing, drying, irradiation, and vacuum and modified-atmosphere packing, enhance the shelf life of products and further reduce last minute operations. On the other hand, new types of equipment have given the baking process in restaurant kitchens a new lease of life. Suppliers of pre-prepared dough cooperate with the manufacturers of specialized ovens so that restaurant staff are required to do nothing more than place the dough in the ovens, activate the appropriate computer programme and remove the bread when it is ready.

But the tendency of these innovations is to transform restaurant kitchens into assembly lines, with fewer staff members, since both the simple repetitive tasks, such as vegetable preparation, and the more complex, last minute operations, will be outsourced. Both the HEREIU and the

IUF argue that "regenerated pre-processed foods" require fewer skills of kitchen staff and result in the loss of many kinds of food preparation and cooking jobs in the industry.

The IUF also points to a devaluation in wages as a result of the deskilling of the remaining jobs. These arguments are difficult to refute, since most of these technologies provide savings in terms of staffing levels. On the other hand, the technologies could open up crucial empowerment possibilities, freeing staff to deal more attentively with customers, thus enhancing the profile of the establishment.

Access to on-line booking via the Internet is causing traditional travel agents considerable problems. It will soon be possible to reserve travel tickets using new mobile phone technology, without the need for a computer. A recent survey carried out by the International Air Transport Association (IATA) revealed that some 37 per cent of travellers worldwide had used electronic tickets, while in the United States, 50 per cent of travellers expected to use such tickets by the end of 2000.

Some travel agents are responding to this situation by adopting a more entrepreneurial attitude, charging customers a fee instead of the traditional commission earned on a ticket price. However, while agents may retain business contracts, they are likely to lose individual customer business for simple trips, and this drop in trade will have an impact on employment levels in the branch. Other agencies see the future in strengthening their role as consultants capable of planning complicated trips involving numerous and varied travel means and stop-offs.

However, while the human element will not disappear, it will probably diminish with the spread of 24-hour "warehouse" travel agents which allow customers to call and make their bookings at any time. According to a 1996 survey by the European Foundation for the Improvement of Living and Working Conditions covering 15 European Union countries, working conditions within the industry included a number of potentially problematic areas, such as irregular working hours, frequent work on Sundays, wages without a fixed basic element in 25 per cent of cases, widespread absence of overtime payments and wage levels generally 20 per cent below the European Union average.

In New Orleans in the United States, the Hospitality, Hotels and Restaurant Organizing Council (HOTROC) has stated that an average hotel housekeeper earns US$5.48 an hour, which places most hotel workers and their families 20 per cent below the federal poverty level. In this connection it should be noted that hotel workers in New Orleans are the only non-unionized hospitality workers in a major United States tourist and convention destination.

In Canada, average weekly earnings increased by 5 per cent in the accommodation sector between 1998 and 1999, but food and beverage earnings lag far behind, having risen by only 1.9 per cent, in line with inflation. The average weekly wage in Canada in accommodation is Can$309.14, and in food and beverage Can$221.30. These wages should be viewed against the national average wage of Can$582.85 a week.

Basic wages reflect competitive labour markets, collective agreements and national laws. Variable pay is emerging as a way to reward employees whose performance enhances the success of an establishment. As a strategy, this idea is not yet common in the sector, but it is beginning to take hold. In the United States, Rodeway Inn International, at Orlando, and Motel Properties, Inc. have both developed successful techniques to reward employees above their basic salaries, based on a monthly assessment scheme.

Turnover figures vary from region to region within countries, but the overall picture is alarming. In the United States, according to a 1998 study, annual turnover in 1997 was running at 51.7 per cent for line-level employees, 11.9 per cent for supervisory levels, and 13.5 per cent for property managers. In Asia, rates of around 30 per cent annually are quoted, rising to more than 50 per cent in Hong Kong, China.

In the United Kingdom, a study carried out by the Institute of Personnel and Development in 1997 found a national turnover rate in the sector of 42 per cent, second only to the retail trade, with a rate of 43.5 per cent and far in advance of construction, where the rate was 25 per cent. In the fast food sector, in both Europe and the United States, turnover rates as high as 300 per cent are reported. It should be noted, however, that turnover figures do not separate out non-standard, part-time jobs from full-time posts.

Many employees, such as college students, are not interested in permanent positions. An American Hotel Foundation report puts the cost of replacement of hourly employees at between US$3,000 and US$10,000, while the average figure for restaurant employees is similar, at US$5,000. Many companies equate the cost of losing a trained manager with roughly one year's salary, allowing for the time it takes for the replacement to become fully operational.

In the United Kingdom, the 1997 report by the Institute of Personnel and Development estimated the cost of replacing a worker in the hotel and leisure industry at £1,922, and concluded that an average of ten weeks was required for training.

Recent negotiations within the European Union in the context of the employer-driven search for greater flexibility at work raise the prospect of improved conditions for part-time and fixed-term contract workers. The European Trade Union Confederation (ETUC) has made clear its position that if employers require more flexibility, then workers must have better protection. The Union of Industrial and Employers' Confederations of Europe (UNICE), which represents private-sector employers, has said that employers are prepared to discuss discrimination against agency workers, provided that the unions recognize that temporary work is an integral part of a functioning market.

The UNICE has also called for an easing of restrictions to allow shorter contracts and greater flexibility in their renewal. The ETUC has observed that temporary agency work is increasing all over the European Union. It doubled between 1996 and 1998 in Spain, while in France and Germany it increased by 30 per cent in three years.

Employers' representatives generally consider that turnover in the industry should be attributed to the essentially transient nature of part of the workforce, namely students, young mothers and young people as a whole, as well as to the general difficulty in retaining staff. Employees, on the other hand, frequently cite low pay as a reason for changing employment, although lack of a career structure and benefits would appear to be of even greater importance.

In the United States, for example, even if hotels and restaurants pay US$12.00 an hour, they are in competition with such jobs as bank tellers, and restaurant work retains the stigma of being physical work. Job stability, career prospects and reasonable hours of work are all part of the equation. As long as other jobs offer equal levels of pay, but more advantageous working and employment conditions, the problem of turnover will persist in the hotel and restaurant sector, unless the industry can create equivalent conditions or compensate in other ways. The transparency provided by the Internet will only serve to highlight these factors as they become more widely known.

In France, Dégriftours, a travel agency that is 100 per cent electronically operated, has applied the 35-hour legislation in France since 1 June 2000. Teams have been increased by 10 per cent to compensate, while the working day has been reduced to 6.8 hours, with seven hours paid. The agency is open from 8 a.m. to 7 p.m., seven days a week, and operates flexibly. This system has been favourably received by staff, who can, for example, choose to work on Sundays and take Wednesdays off in order to care for children.

There is also a rotation of weekend work to ensure a fair distribution of the less social working hours. The tour operator Nouvelles Frontières has reached a different agreement after nine months of negotiation. The company has signed an agreement to increase its staff by 8 per cent with the help of state subsidies. Employees will be able to organize their working time according to one of three formulas, namely a four-day week without reduction in pay, a four-and-a-half-day week, or a five-day, 40-hour week yielding 28 extra leave days.

The employees must decide on one of the formulas for a period of one year, planned in advance with their supervisors in the services and agencies. The French fast food sector signed an agreement on 15 April 1999 effectively reducing the working week to 35 hours as of 1 November 1999. This could create between 2,000 and 3,000 new jobs in a sector that employs 80,000 people in France. A national agreement signed on 1 April 1999 also reduced the working week to 35 hours for amusement park employees, with no loss of pay.

Moreover, the 35-hour week is being implemented by some employers in the French institutional catering market. In the United Kingdom, the British Hospitality Association (BHA) claims that the new European Union Working Time Directive restricts working hours although there is no evidence that staff want them restricted. The BHA argues that the 11-hour obligatory break between shifts may cause problems for hotels with receptionists who like to see guests in at night and out in the morning, and for kitchen and restaurant staff serving dinner and breakfast.

A number of negotiated workload reductions have emerged recently in Europe and North America. In the institutional catering sector of the Netherlands, a recently negotiated national collective agreement provides for a 10 per cent annual reduction in workloads based on evaluations at the workplace. Procedures are to be established for handling workload-related grievances, and temporary contracts must now state the actual number of hours worked. The possibility of early retirement at 61 years with 80 per cent pay is included in the agreement.

While the chances of contracting or communicating HIV are minimal in the industry, training is needed to assuage personnel fears and make staff aware of the risks that do exist. In terms of employment, the disease may have an impact on three major areas of a business: productivity, employee benefits and morale. The establishment of an HIV policy within an enterprise is therefore a necessity, irrespective of the level of HIV infection in individual countries. In respect of workers who become infected, a number of good practices have come to the fore over recent years.

For example, if a worker is HIV-infected, employers should: accept a less than ideal level of performance, as long as minimum standards are met; modify the employee's job description or reassign the employee to a different job; allow more time off for health appointments; allow more sick leave or absenteeism (with or without pay); arrange a more flexible work schedule, or provide for the employee to switch to part-time work, or allow the employee to work from home.

As a means of lowering costs, a growing management trend has been to subcontract various services in the industry, such as food and beverages, housekeeping, laundry services, security and valeting. Hotels are increasingly grouping together to employ a common Internet reservation system provider, resulting in a reduction in jobs in the hotels concerned.

Hotels are also leasing out their restaurants, particularly in the food and beverage market segment. This implies a severe drop in union membership if the employees of the outsourced companies are non-union members. The New York-New York Casino in Las Vegas in the United States has outsourced virtually all its food and beverage operations to the Ark Restaurants Corporation.

The nature of many jobs in the tourism industry creates an atypical employment relationship and special working conditions, such as flexible working time and temporary or part-time work. In addition, there is a general demand by enterprises for greater flexibility in working relations, so as to increase productivity in the now only a "dot-com away".

The Swiss trade journal, "Expresso", defines casual workers as those who are employed on an occasional and irregular basis in connection with specific short-term requirements. In Switzerland, the casual worker has the same legal rights as a full- or part-time worker, and the only difference lies in the fact that holidays may be paid in the form of a 10.65 per cent supplement to the hourly wage for regimes allowing five weeks' annual holiday, or an 8.33 per cent supplement for regimes of four weeks' annual holiday. A similar system prevails in France.

A hotel in London has sought to solve the problem of irregular workload peaks by employing university students on a part-time basis for a fixed number of hours annually, in this instance 500 hours, which can be used as required, with students able to exchange hours among themselves according to their individual availability. According to the IUF, the need for labour flexibility has always given rise to problems in respect of maintenance of permanent staffing levels in the hospitality industry, and there is a very high proportion of part-time and casual work compared to other industries.

In Austria, there is a 26 per cent seasonal variation in employment in the sector; in Spain the figure is 47 per cent; in Italy it is more than 50 per cent, while in

Denmark the number of employees in the sector doubles during the summer season. Part-time work has also been growing faster than full-time employment in the service sector in Australia, where its incidence is relatively high by international standards, particularly among women.

Although part-time labour has been used frequently in the Netherlands, employers have recently sought to retain more full-time personnel: the figures show a reduction of temporary and seasonal employees from 82,100 in 1995 to 67,100 in 1997, and a corresponding increase in permanent full-time contracts from 132,500 to 160,300. In the rest of Europe, the incidence of part-time employment is increasing.

In Italy, part-time contracts in restaurants have increased by 80 per cent over the same two-year period and by almost 30 per cent in hotels. The 1995 Joint ECF-IUF Declaration on Flexibility of Labour and Organization of Working Time, Part-time Work and the Creation of Jobs, while stating that the creation of full-time jobs is a priority, lists a number of advantages which part-time work may present for both employers and workers.

Such employment may correspond to the needs of certain groups of workers - students, parents wishing to accommodate family responsibilities, workers in need of time for training or a flexible transition to retirement through reduced working time. It may also provide a means of reintegration into the labour market for the long-term unemployed. On the other hand, there is the risk that such employment may lead to the creation of a kind of secondary labour market, lacking the same levels of social security cover as a result of minimum hourly thresholds for access to entitlements including training, proportionately lower pay, and the inability of these employees to participate in the collective bargaining process.

Moreover, regulatory attempts by governments to create employment by reducing the charges payable on part-time labour can encourage over-reliance on such labour, to the detriment of full-time jobs. In Australia, research in 1996 showed that casual workers accounted for over 50 per cent of employees in the industry. The unions responded by advocating the replacement of casual jobs with permanent, part-time posts, thus seeking an improvement in, rather than the elimination of, part-time work.

The rates of pay received by casual employees remained higher than those paid to permanent part-time workers, but did not include benefits such as paid holidays. Some employees enjoyed the very wide degree of flexibility offered by casual employment, while for employers it presented the advantage of allowing them to dismiss employees without a period of notice. As a result of union activity, some industry agreements were reached, containing an explicit management and union commitment to convert casual hours to permanent, part-time hours, but enforcement has remained limited.

Although hotel, restaurant and catering workers may have to work irregular hours, they reportedly have an increasing choice available to them. A law has also recently been passed according to which workers have the right under certain conditions to switch to part-time work should they choose to do so. In areas where the seasonal element of the trade is particularly marked, and where the hotels or restaurants will only function during a limited period of the year, tourist establishments are obliged to close during the low season, with many of the staff, including hotel and restaurant owners, drawing unemployment benefit.

The Scottish winter sports centre at Aviemore has made considerable headway in countering this problem by promoting itself as a centre for "green" tourism and an ideal base from which to explore the surrounding Cairngorm region. The area has undertaken this promotion in partnership with conservation societies to ensure the sustainability of the venture, and much of the business now takes place during the summer months.

3

Opportunites and Challenges of Tourism

New Challenges of Indian Tourism

Tourism is currently one of the major segments of Indian economy. It is fast emerging as the industry of the twenty-first century, with its substantial contributions to sustainable human development, including poverty alleviation, employment generation, environmental regeneration and advancement of women.

Tourism has also become an instrument for the promotion of handicrafts, arts and the cultural heritage of country. Direct employment in the tourism sector during 1997-1998 was estimated to have been about 13.8 million, while total employment including indirect employment due to tourism amounted to 32.57 million.

A large percentage of that figure was generated in backward and remote areas. The employment generation capacity of tourism industries per unit of investment is also one of the highest in the country. International tourist arrivals during 1999 totaled 2.48 million. Foreign exchange earnings from tourism during 1999 was estimated to have been $US 2,916.79 million.

Recognizing the importance of tourism as a socio-economic activity and a major contributor to the national economy, the development of the sector is being given high priority. The government has formulated a new National Tourism Policy that emphasizes the roles of the public and private sectors in tourism development.

The policy also recognizes the importance of creating awareness and the participation of grass-roots level institutions in tourism development. Keeping in view the required level of sustainability to be achieved in the development of tourism, particularly in ecologically fragile areas, the government has also introduced a comprehensive policy and guidelines for the development of ecotourism in the country.

The tourism industry at present is handicapped by inadequacies in the basic infrastructural facilities as well as a lack of adequate incentives for investment in the sector. These issues are being addressed in a selective manner by taking up integrated tourism development projects. Tourism is expected to become the top foreign exchange earner and the most important industry in terms of employment generation.

Tourism in India has been projected as the biggest industry of the future. Tourism creates income and employment. It also develops backward regions, revives traditional handicrafts and art, while contributing to national integration and international understanding. Although tourism is very important, national governments by and large do not include it in economic development planning. It is not even a priority item in sectoral budget allocations in many countries.

In India, in the budgeting process, tourism earnings are grouped under the heading of "invisible". The impact of tourism is invisible because too many activities form links in the chain and a system does not exist for properly identifying those links. The World Travel and Tourism Council (WTTC) has identified more than 30 sectors as the "core" of the tourism business. It is of crucial importance, therefore, to have a common definition for measuring the impact.

It should include all the "ripple" effects and should provide the means of devising a comparable yardstick. Tourism Satellite Accounts (TSA) has been used by many countries to focus on the economic importance of tourism. The 1991 Ottawa Declaration, followed by the United Nations conference in 1993 on the subject, pointed attention towards the importance of the issues involved. France began using TSA in 1988, and Canada, the United States, Singapore, Poland, among others, have made substantial progress in the meantime.

The Organization for Economic Cooperation and Development (OECD) also developed guidelines for TSAs. The World Tourism Organization has also supported preliminary activities towards this end in other countries. WTTC recently conducted a pilot study in India that foresaw tourism in providing 6 per cent to GDP in 10 years compared with the current 1.8 per cent.

Since India's GDP is large, that increase will make a great difference. The World. Tourism Organization needs to collate these experiences and cull the salient points in order to formulate a common yardstick for all to follow. A set of statistics based on international comparability is needed that will allow a uniform international comparison. A single consistently defined format needs to be developed.

Credible numbers are required so that a hard economic case can be made for facilitating political decision-making and providing due place for tourism in the public policy process. Precise definitions and classifications are necessary because tourism is multidimensional and covers diverse elements.

Once the conceptual framework has been finalized, implementing it will require state policy to play a role. All organizational and system changes will need to be carefully managed. Most functionaries under a particular system are resistant to changes. Therefore, motivation will be necessary. To avoid resistance, the new system will have to be built around the existing one.

The World Tourism Organization Action Plan must give priority to training, the development of uniform manuals and training guides, and regional and national seminars and workshops. The public and private sectors must be involved in the process.

Tourism consists of a range of products and services consumed by visitors. These are provided by a multitude of establishments and agencies functioning at various levels. The infrastructure for tourism consists not only of on-site facilities such as hotels, restaurants, entertainment facilities, etc., but also includes all forms of transport and communication infrastructure and basic amenities.

The provision of an integrated system of physical infrastructure, including air, rail and road services, water supply, drainage and solid waste disposal systems is thus a prerequisite for the development of tourism. All departments and agencies involved in tourism infrastructure development must, therefore, adopt a joint approach and establish synergy in such efforts.

The Ministry of Tourism is in the process of formulating a new tourism policy aimed at achieving necessary linkages and synergies in the policies and programmes of concerned departments and agencies by establishing effective coordination mechanisms at the central, state and district levels. The focus of the policy will be to develop tourism as a common endeavour by all the agencies directly concerned at the central and state levels, for both public and private sector undertakings.

International air-sea capacity involves two main objectives:

— Assessing air seat capacity and load factors in terms of both sector and seasonal requirements, and augmenting capacity in the critical sectors.

— Improving accessibility and promoting arrivals at destinations of interest by opening up airports at important tourist centers for charter flights.

In the case of airports, two main objectives are envisaged:

— Conversion of more and more airports to international status and standard.

— Modernizing and improving arrival and departure lounges at the country's international airports.

Domestic air services, involves making better use of domestic air services by:

— Improving accessibility to more tourist centers by introducing services of small aircraft and helicopters.

— Converting Guwahati Airport into a regional hub and introducing services using small aircraft to all the tourist centers in the north-eastern region of India.

The improvement of the rail service will include:

— Developing comprehensive rail circuits connecting important tourist destinations.

— Extending the railway network to connect important tourist centres.

— Improving hygiene, the environment and passenger facilities in and around the railway stations serving important tourist centres.

Three main objectives are envisaged in the effort to better utilize the road network:

— Providing modern wayside amenities on the highways connecting important tourist centres.

— Providing standard signage on roads leading to tourist spots.

— Ensuring uninterrupted inter-state movement of tourist coaches and vehicles through the rationalization of taxes.

Maintenance of Heritage Sites and improvement of tourist facilities, will include:

— Ensuring proper maintenance and professional site management of important tourist attractions and monuments.

— Involving local authorities, trusts, etc., in the restoration and preservation of tourist attractions and the maintenance of their surroundings.

Under product development, four main objectives are envisaged:

— Giving guidance and financial assistance to State/Union Territory governments in preparing tourism master plans, identifying tourism resources, and setting priorities for development activities and projects.

— Involving the town and country planning agencies in the integration of area development plans with tourism development.

— Focusing on the development of ecotourism in the north-east and the Himalayan States as well as various islands.

— Developing places of pilgrimage by providing the requisite infrastructural facilities in order to promote domestic and international pilgrimage tourism.

Private sector investment in the tourism industry

As a consequence of economic restructuring and liberalization of policies, the tourism industry of India has been declared a priority sector for foreign investment. The horizons for foreign investment in the tourism sector were widened and it has been eligible for automatic approval of foreign direct investment up to 51 per cent of the equity since July 1991.

Higher foreign equity participation in specific cases is also allowed on a case-by-case basis. Non-resident India investment of up to 100 per cent is allowed. Automatic approvals are given for foreign technology agreements and management contracts within specified parameters.

Tourism is the second largest net foreign exchange earner by way of invisible exports. Tourism creates more jobs for every rupee invested than any other sector. It also creates jobs at the local level, dispensing with the need for migration to distant areas of the country in order to find a livelihood.

In fact, tourism plays a major role in promoting large-scale employment opportunities. Keeping in view all these factors, the government has accorded export house status to the tourism industry. All hotels, travel agents, tour operators and tourist transport operators are now entitled to recognition as an export house, trading house, star trading house or super star trading house.

Earning foreign exchange entitles them to certain benefits. This approach will go a long way in assisting the promotion of, and attracting investment in, tourism. The aim of the government is to achieve sustained growth of tourist facilities in the private sector and to ensure high standards of quality are maintained in the delivery of services.

Tourism has therefore been given the status of an industry and several incentives have been made available, both by the central and state governments. The incentives provided by the central government include:

— An interest subsidy of 3 per cent on loans from financial institutions is available for hotel projects in the one-star to three-star categories of hotel projects outside metropolitan cities.

— A subsidy of 5 per cent is available for such hotel projects if they are located within the travel circuits and destinations identified for intensive development under the National Action Plan for Tourism. Heritage

Hotel projects are eligible for a 5 per cent interest subsidy.

— As a fiscal incentive, 50 per cent of the foreign exchange profits derived by hotels, travel agents and tour operators are exempt from income tax. The balance in foreign exchange is also exempt provided it is reinvested in tourism projects.

Hotels located in rural areas, hilly areas and places of pilgrimage are allowed an income tax exemption of 50 per cent on their profits. Hotels located in other areas are allowed a 30 per cent exemption. This privilege is not, however, applicable to hotels located in metropolitan cities.

Imports of special items for the hotel industry are permitted, subject to import entitlement. Concessional customs duty rates are charged for imports of specified goods required in the initial setting up or substantial expansion of hotels.

An Export Promotion Capital Goods Scheme has been introduced for the service sector. The scheme includes hotels and restaurants, travel agents and tour operators. Under the scheme, capital goods can be imported at a concessional duty rate of 10 per cent, subject to the fulfillment of an expert obligation over a period of time.

Tourism Development in Bangladesh

Tourists are attracted by various natural and manmade objects. Among these are sea beaches, archaeological and historical relics, flora and fauna, natural scenery, tribal lifestyles and the indigenous culture. There is an abundance of these types of attractions in Bangladesh.

However, so far no definite or coordinated steps have been taken in Bangladesh to increase national income in foreign currency by developing these potential and internationally recognizable attractions. Following the independence of Bangladesh, tourism development plans were prepared with foreign assistance.

The latest five-year development plan and other perspective plans on tourism development were prepared with assistance from the World Tourism Organization (WTO) and the United Nations Development Programme (UNDP). Domestic private sector investments in the development of this industry have been made in an uncoordinated manner, so they have not achieved any remarkable progress.

The development of the tourism industry has been constrained for these reasons and it has not been possible to earn the desired amount of foreign currency or to create employment opportunities that this sector could provide. It has also not been possible to attract domestic and foreign investment into the tourism industry due to the lack of proper development in this sector. In addition, it has not been possible to create opportunities to improve and uphold the international image of Bangladesh people and the population has thus been deprived of recreational facilities.

Bangladesh has enough resources to enable it to become a major tourist destination. Its big rivers, mangrove forests, beaches and eye-catching hills and dales in the south and south-east of the country offer great potential. In addition to this wide range of natural resources, Bangladesh has a rich and diversified cultural heritage and areas with tribal lifestyles and natural beauty.

Economic benefits of tourism

It is widely recognized that tourism can play a very important role in the economy of a developing country. Besides improvement in the balance of payments, it generates many other socio-economic benefits including the expansion of economic activities and employment opportunities. Bangladesh is a developing country and still faces many difficulties. The country has achieved political sovereignty, but economic freedom has yet to be gained. In seeking the goal of self-reliance, tourism can definitely contribute to developing countries such as Bangladesh.

Tourism development can provide a significant contribution to the national economy. The direct and indirect benefits to the national economy may be achieved in similar or even better ways than in other sectors of the economy. In the productive industries or agro-based industries, several investments have been made. The results have shown that returns on investments in those industries may be reasonable but never lucrative.

The tourism industry, however, offers an avenue of investment that can ensure a better and lucrative return, thus contributing more to the national economy. Tourism has always been developed as a multilateral industry. Unlike other productive industries, it has wide range of inputs and, as a result, expenditures on inputs are distributed more widely than in most traditional industries. The resultant distribution of wealth creates a higher multiplier effect in the economy.

Moreover, the tourism industry offers a variety of choices. For example, a tourist may like to buy some product or visit a part of the country. The wider circulation of money through so many sellers will have an obviously greater multiplier effect in the economy. There is, of course, no specific calculation of this effect as yet, but according to a report prepared by the World Tourism Organization in 1990, the multiplier effect in the tourism sector was 1:5. Nevertheless, with the advent of a variety of choices, this effect is much higher in Bangladesh at present.

Since the tourism industry requires a series of inputs that are varied in nature, it automatically opens up a wide range of economic activities in different professions and different areas. For example, establishment of a hotel in certain areas calls for regular supply of many items and as a result economic activities for production and supply of those items automatically grows up there.

The wide variety of choices by the visiting tourists also calls for variety of supplies from different areas thus creating a chain of economic activities. Tourism is mostly a service industry. Therefore, it is more labour oriented than other sectors of production. Automated and computerized processes may replace human beings in other industries to a great extent, but in the tourism sector, the key factor is service, particularly personal service.

Moreover, the wide variety of choices in tourism very seldom allow automation. It is, therefore, clear that the tourism industry offers more employment opportunities than other industries. It is a fact that with the unbalanced growth of population in the country, the problem of unemployment is acute. Thus, in view of the fact that Bangladesh has a labour-intensive economy the creation of more employment opportunities is essential.

The tourism industry can create employment opportunities and a productive labour force to a greater degree than other sectors. Services and facilities being the main products of the tourism industry, taxation and other levies on consumer goods, especially luxury products, will be more beneficial to a country such as Bangladesh. Taxation on tourism consumption, especially on luxury products and services, will not greatly affect the local population, while on the other hand it will contribute a great deal to the national budget.

The development of infrastructure facilities is a prerequisite for a developing country. Tourism development provides these facilities. The needed infrastructure for tourist facilities is also useful to non-tourists. Furthermore, transportation facilities such as car or boat rental in the tourism industry adds considerably to the national communication system. Specialization in tourism transport facilities also improves the overall standard of transport services.

Attempts are being made to export non-traditional products such as handicrafts, souvenirs and other cottage industry products. Several organizations are also putting great effort into popularizing and marketing these products abroad. Cottage industries are showing spontaneous growth in every village of Bangladesh and are playing a very important role in the national economy. But the most striking problem is improving the marketability of such products.

Tourism obviously offers better marketing opportunities and better prices, thus encouraging production and the growth of small industries. Recreation and holidaying help to develop the mental well being of people and improve work efficiency. In a labour-intensive economy such as Bangladesh, work efficiency is a vital factor in enhancing overall production.

Tourism is an excellent way of achieving such benefits due to its very wide range of recreational activities. With the development of tourism, the culture of Bangladesh would gain extensive international recognition. This, in turn, would result in greater domestic awareness, further development and a broader outlook. The archaeological sites in Bangladesh bear testimony to its glorious past. The many temples and mosques, shrines, music and festivals could provide pleasure and knowledge to people from far and wide.

The educational and moral values accruing from such cultural tourism would contribute extensively to socio-economic improvement of the country. Tourism also offers wide regional and international linkages. As a result, more international and regional organizations are offering the country wider participation in tourism-related forums. Bangladesh, with its limited financial resources, depends much on foreign assistance.

International cooperation and foreign assistance can be equally sought in the tourism development of Bangladesh. The tourism industry is potentially a major source of foreign exchange, contributing considerably to a favourable balance of payments. In Bangladesh, however, there are many exports that earn foreign exchange, but in all cases it involves the physical transfer of goods.

However, tourism is mostly a service industry, involving minimal physical transfer of goods and services. People from other countries visit Bangladesh, enjoy the facilities, spend foreign exchange and return home. Except for purchases of gifts and souvenirs, tourism consumption involves services and facilities; there is very little to be physically transferred. For a country such as Bangladesh, which has little surplus for exports, this characteristic of tourism can play a vital role.

There is good potential for the development of tourism in Bangladesh as it has natural scenic spots and long stretches of beach, ancient mosques, temples, monuments, etc. Due to the lack of integrated policy and programmes, infrastructure facilities and publicity, these potentials have not fully been exploited.

In the fifth Five-Year Plan, emphasis will be given to the development of integrated tourism facilities in order to attract both domestic and foreign tourists. Attempts will be made to develop physical facilities in the hill tracts, coastal areas, and peripheral areas of Mymensingh, Bogra, Dinajpur and Sylhet. The government will create an attractive environment for the private sector to invest in the development of physical facilities and resorts.

The development of low-cost integrated tourism facilities in north-eastern areas, the Chittagong Hill Tracts, coastal areas and hilly districts. The implementation of priority programmes and projects in accordance with the Tourism Master Plan that has already been prepared. Tourism sites will be developed in collaboration with other sectors such as transport and communications, hotels, motels and catering establishments, etc.

The private sector and non-governmental organizations will be encouraged to develop and run tourism sites and other facilities. The construction of a tourist motel and recreation center at Bandarban, the district headquarters of the Bandarban Hill Tracts, 92 kilometres from Chittagong by metalled road at the estimated cost: foreign exchange valued at Taka 1,000 million ($US 20 million).

The construction of a tourist motel and recreation center at Khagrachari, the district headquarters of the Khagrachari Hill Tracts, 117 kilometres to the north of Chittagong by metalled road at the estimated cost: foreign exchange valued at Taka 1,000 million ($US 20 million).

Bangladesh, as a vacation destination, has many facets. It is endowed with almost all the natural potentials that attract tourist. These include: Cox's Bazaar, the longest unbroken clean and sandy beach in the world; Sundarbans, the home of the majestic Royal Bengal tigers, Dhaka, the capital known as the city of mosques and muslin; Rangamati, the heart of the panoramic lake district; Sylhet, land of fascinating hills and tea gardens; Chittagong, the largest port city of the country and known as the city of shrines; Mainamati, Mahasthangarh and Paharpur, archaeological treasures of Hindu and Buddhist rule in the country from 300 BC to 1200 AD.

The Bangladesh Parjatan Corporation (BPC) was established in 1973 with the dual responsibility of the development and promotion of tourism in the country. BPC has renovated existing tourist facilities and created new facilities at important tourist spots since it inception. Tourist facilities created so far include hotels, motels, youth hostels, restaurants, duty-free shops and land and water transport at different tourist spots around the country.

BPC accommodation units now have a total capacity of about 800 beds, while the restaurants have a total seating capacity of more than 1,200. BPC has a fleet of 33 commercial land transport vehicles for tourists, and offers city sightseeing tours, package tours and excursion trips. Moreover, it organizes special city sightseeing tours for transit passengers as well as regular river cruises in Dhaka.

However, the existing facilities appear to be inadequate for meeting the evergrowing demand of local and foreign tourists. In order to meet growing demand in the sector, a master plan for tourism development in Bangladesh that was prepared by the World Tourism Organization in coordination with the United Nations Development Programme has already identified potential tourist products and the required capital investment needed to create and expand tourist facilities. Since private capital is not abundant in the field of tourism development in Bangladesh, BPC has to play the leading role as a promoter of the industry.

Basic infrastructure facilities, such as road and rail transport, and electricity and water supplies exist in most of the proposed project areas mentioned above. International investors are always welcome in Bangladesh to participate in the development of proposed tourism projects. There is enough justification and many positive factors to make investment in tourism worthwhile in Bangladesh.

Bangladesh is a developing country, and therefore, its economy does not permit huge investments in the development of infrastructural facilities in identified areas for tourist development. The government, therefore, requested ESCAP to carry out a feasibility study in order to explore the possibilities of getting financing from the World Bank/Asian Development Bank/donor countries, etc. But the main impediment is the lack of priority given to the tourism sector in Bangladesh.

The government is therefore taking appropriate measures to attach due priority in the tourism sector so that economic benefits can be realized as has been done in other countries. In addition to unhealthy trade unionism, political unrest and lack of political commitment in Bangladesh, and procedural delays due to the bureaucratic administration in every sector, there is rampant corruption that actually discourages foreign investment in the country.

Inadequate funding by the government in the tourism sector is also a major impediment to tourism infrastructure development. Suggested measures for creating a favourable atmosphere for investment in tourism infrastructure and expanding economic benefits of tourism. There could be three different categories of investment for expanding the economic benefits of tourism:

(a) 100 per cent foreign ownership, including Bangladeshi nationals ordinarily resident abroad;

(b) joint ventures between foreign and Bangladeshi entrepreneurs resident in Bangladesh;

(c) 100 per cent Bangladesh ownership among those resident in Bangladesh.

Investment in convertible foreign currencies by foreign investors, and the option to establish public/private limited companies or sole proprietorship concerns, could be allowed. The Foreign Private Investment (Promotion and Protection) Act 1980 guarantees the security of all foreign investment in such projects in ETN. OPIC's insurance and finance programmes are available. Security and safeguards under the Multilaterai Investment Guarantee Agency (MIGA) needs to be ensured. The arbitration facility of the International Centre for the Settlement of Investment Disputes (ICSID) also needs to be involved.

Telex, fax and international dialing services, e-mail and Internet connections through a satellite system need to be made available in the Exclusive Tourist Zones (ETZs). Adequate communication services through sea, rail, road and air should be ensured where possible and necessary. The provision of facilities should include:

(a) making land available on a rental/lease basis for a reasonable ploughback period;

(b) electricity, telecommunications, gas and water supplies provided by the ETZs;

(c) import permits and work permits for foreign nationals to be issued;

(d) an ETZ to be a secure and protected area;

(e) recreational facilities allowed or made available;

(f) availability of food and beverages allowed on payment of a nominal tax by foreigners working in an ETZ;

(g) simplification of procedural requirements; and

(h) granting of permanent residentship to foreign citizens investing sizable amounts.

New Oppotunities of Tourism Development in Cambodia

Cambodia is part of South-East Asia, where the "East Asian Miracle" has taken place in less than two decades. With a robust and higher than world average economic growth in the region, there are vast opportunities in markets for technology, infrastructure investment and consumer goods.

Being in the Asian and Pacific region, interregional trade will expand even further. It is often said that successive waves have pushed and pulled the East Asian Miracle, starting with Japan, followed by China, France, Taiwan province of China, the United States, Association of South East Asian Nations (ASEAN) members and European countries.

Although there was serious decline of 16 per cent in tourist arrivals in 1997, Cambodia was still able to attract and maintain an average 20 per cent annual increase in arrivals between 1993 and 1997. According to current statistics, tourist arrivals in the first half of 1998 were 35 per cent lower than in the same period in 1997. However, the tourist arrivals in the first half of 1998 were 30 per cent higher than the last six months of 1997.

Overall, tourist arrivals in 1998 showed a slight decrease compared with 1997. In the first half of 1999, tourist arrivals by air increased, if compared with the total of 1998 from 175,910 to 233,597. The Ministry of Tourism is targeting an increase of 20 to 25 per cent tourist arrivals in year 2000 and 2001.

In 1995, the gross domestic product (GDP) of Cambodia was estimated to be about $US 2.8 billion, which translates into a per capita income of approximately $US 280. This ranks the country as one of the least developed in Asia. The Asian Development Bank's Economic Review summarized the socio-economic situation in Cambodia as follows:

"Cambodia is one of the world's poorest countries with income per capita of about $US 252 in 1994 and it is ranked 147 among 173 countries in the world, based on the Human Development index, according to the Human Development Report, 1994 prepared by the United Nations Development Programme (UNDP). Income disparities are wide with the highest decile (highest 10 per cent of the population), accounting for more than half on the country's income. There are no official estimates of poverty in Cambodia, but it is generally accepted as being in excess of 60 per cent and concentrated in the rural areas where 85.90 per cent of the population lives".

The United Nations Transitional Authority in Cambodia (UNTAC) really "jumpstarted" the Cambodia economy in 1992/1993, including the development of hotels, restaurants and related enterprises, to serve the large influx of UNTAC personnel. The international community has responded well with donor support, and both local and foreign investment in economic activities and infrastructure development has been attracted.

Much of the economic activity has, however, been focused on Phnom Penh and, to a lesser extent, Sihanoukville and Siem Reap. The economy is dominated by agriculture and services, while industry plays a minor though increasingly important role. Hotels, restaurants and other tourism sector enterprises are estimated to contribute about 1.8 per cent of GDP, although this does not capture the full extent of tourist spending in the retail trade and transportation.

Tourist expenditures in Cambodia represent a major injection of money into the economy, stimulating a variety of economic activities. Because the economy is a relatively open one, there is no measure available from the banking system as to the amount of foreign exchange being earned from tourism. In fact, much of the urban economy is operating in US dollars. Also to be considered is that many of these activities are fuelled not only by tourists, but also by the large number of expatriates working long-term in the country.

Total tourist expenditures were estimated to be about $US 100 million in 1995 and approximately $US 143 million in 1998. Tourism is making a substantial contribution to GDP, based on calculating the multiplier effect of tourism. The estimated $US 101 million of tourist expenditure in 1995 would have produced $US 47 million in direct income, $US 57 million in indirect revenue and a total of $US 153 million in direct, indirect and induced income.

In the 1990s and beyond, Cambodia is the right place to be for business investment. There are excellent opportunities in labour-intensive industries, such as tourism, garments and textiles, light and electronic industries, agriculture and aquaculture, and infrastructure development. All of these sectors are growing rapidly. Malaysia is currently the largest investor in Cambodia, followed by the Republic of Korea, Singapore, Taiwan province of China, Europe and the Americas. Cambodia welcomes every country.

To date, 35 per cent of investment approved by the Cambodian Investment Board (CIB) has been committed and 65 per cent is pending. The government is considering a comprehensive plan for developing a tourism zone in Siem Reap that replicates the famous temples of Angkor Wat in the north-western region of country. A tourism development zone, covering more than 1,000 ha, has been earmarked for the project, which is expected to attract more than $US 1 billion in foreign investment.

The proposal includes several hotels, commercial, cultural and conference centers, sports facilities, a residential area, a hospital and, ultimately, a museum of contemporary Cambodian art. The major tourism areas at present are Phnom Penh, Siem Reap and Sihanoukville as well some other places with tourism potential that are served or expected to be served both by air and road.

Improvements are planned at Pochentong International Airport at Phnom Penh, and the airports at Sihanoukville and Siem Reap in the near future. Siem Reap airport is also being considered for development as a larger facility within the next 10 years. Other domestic airports will require some improvement in terms of facilities and services as tourism develops in those areas.

A major "Cambodia Transport Rehabilitation Study" co-financed by SIDA and UNDP has been completed. The study includes an analysis and recommendations on road, railways, international ports and inland waterways. It sets forth transportation policies and a detailed rehabilitation programme for 2000 to 2004. When the rehabilitation programme has been completed, good road access to Cambodia and its major cities will be available from neighbouring countries, and to tourism areas within the country. Rehabilitation of the road between Phnom Penh and Sihanoukville is almost complete. Progress is also being made on road rehabilitation between Phnom Penh and Siem Reap and other roads.

The focus for rehabilitation of infrastructure has particularly been on the main urban areas where critical needs exist. Several urban infrastructure studies and an improvement programme have been carried out. In the case of Phnom Penh, international assistance programmes are either underway or proposed for improving all aspects of the urban infrastructure (roads, water and electric power supplies, waste management, telecommunications and drainage), which will serve tourism development as well as general urban needs.

The major tourism development plan proposed for Siem Reap focuses on infrastructure to serve tourism. In planning for tourism, it is important to take into account major investment projects related to tourism that are underway or proposed. Several of the major hotel projects underway are referred to above. In addition, major integrated tourism development projects have been proposed for Sihanoukville and Siem Reap.

Cambodia has favourable conditions and rarely faces natural disasters such as floods, storms and earthquakes. Such a favourable conditions ensure that Cambodia has a good climate, wildlife and a wide variety of plants, lakes, beaches, natural beauty and mountains.

Cambodia has natural resources, but important tourism areas have little or no tourism infrastructure, such as sewage disposal systems, electrical and communications systems, water supply and drainage systems, highways, airports, railways, parking lots, parks, night lighting, marinas and dock facilities, bus and train station facilities, resorts, motels, shopping centers, places of entertainment, museums, stores and similar structures, or transportation such as buses, taxis and similar passenger transportation facilities.

In recent years, Cambodia has achieved much in the macroeconomy, qualifying for the General Agreement on Trade and Tariff (GATT) and the Generalized System of Preferences (GSP). In October 1996, Cambodia was also granted Most Favoured Nation (MFN) status by the United States. Cambodia has unique natural endowments of large forest resources and agricultural potential, and very large, but untapped offshore resources. This offers enormous scope for tourism. All that is required is investment and sustainable exploitation.

Cambodia provides low labour costs with a young and willing work force that is disciplined, ready to learn and quick to apply state-of-the-art technology. The government is enhancing the education and training of the population, which will boost the capacity of this most vital resource of the nation. Starting virtually with a clean slate, Cambodia is absorbing and adjusting rapidly to modern technology in all fields including telecommunications and computer technology. Starting at the lower end of the ladder, Cambodia has great potential for enhancing its productivity in all sectors using modern knowledge, while avoiding the pitfalls experienced by others.

The tax system initiated in 1985 imposes taxes on imports and exports, sales and profits, business licenses, and locally-produced goods. In order to raise additional revenue, the authorities introduced additional taxes on sales, profits and rental income in 1994, followed in 1995 by income tax on wages and salaries, unutilized land and specific goods, property transfer tax and stamp duty.

In promoting the tourism industry, Cambodia has to depend on attracting resources by focusing on its natural resources and cultural traditions together with its tremendous potential for tourism. We take pride in our wealth of natural resources, but have been unable to do much in developing the necessary tourism infrastructure due to the lack of investment resources. However, urgent development is needed in certain areas, such as:

— *Infrastructure* - building and renovating more roads and public facilities, restaurants, electricity and water supplies, etc.

— *Service systems* - providing/adequate and efficient telecommunication system, utilities, public information, etc.

— *Marketing information programmes* - strong support and cooperation is needed from the relevant ministries and international organizations in the consistent implementation of a more rigorous marketing and promotion programme. This is especially important in counterbalancing international media reports about Cambodia as unsafe and insecure.

— *Air transportation services* - more international and regional airports need to be linked with Cambodia, and flights need to be punctual and not so frequently cancelled. Domestic flights and local airline companies need to improve their services. The concession company at Pochentong International Airport in Phnom Penh needs to be more active in implementing its contract signed with the Government.

— *Land transportation services* - traveling by land in Cambodia is very difficult because of the lack of roads connecting major destinations throughout the country. In addition, many of the existing roads need major repairs. Usually, it takes 6-7 hours to travel 200-300 km between major cities in the country.

— *Water transportation services* - despite having the convenience of the Great Lake as well as the Mekong River running though the country, travel by boat is not frequent among tourists or locals. This is due to the inadequate and low standard of water transportation facilities. This situation is also the problem of an unsafe environment. Other constraints to increasing investment in tourism infrastructure in Cambodia include:

— Unfavourable laws and investment process.

— High-priced services.

— A lack of human resources.

— Airport taxes (international and domestic) that are too high compared with other countries.

— A lack of airport services and facilities.

— Accommodation (hotel) rates that are too high, while quality is not on a par with international standards.

— Itineraries of group tours are not as comprehensive and selective as in other countries of the region.

— Environmental concerns.

— Security remains a major issue.

The government has drafted new laws and amended existing ones. In addition, the government is investing or encouraging investment in certain areas. Overall, the Ministry of Tourism and the Government are committed to the tourism industry and are optimistic about efforts to cooperate and take initiatives to play a more active role in the international community.

The Ministry of Tourism and the Government have been working diligently to improve infrastructure, utilities, health facilities, and training and promotional activities in order to improve and help facilitate international travel and the country's tourism industry. At the same time, efforts are being made to expand and improve the investment law, economic law and other related laws.

The Ministry of Tourism is preparing a comprehensive governing and legal system framework for effectively implementing such laws. In addition, the Government has been seeking support from the private sector for investment in improving and building infrastructure. Finally, through support and cooperation from the international community, the private sector and interested governments, Cambodia hopes that its endeavours to emerge as an active player in the world community will soon become a reality.

Moreover, Cambodia hopes that its tourism industry will be a major vehicle for helping to boost the country's economic development and solve the problems that have grown in the past two decades of war. Therefore, the growth of the tourism industry, together with the development of tourism resources, depends on effective promotion. If the tourism industry grows, Cambodia will achieve:

— Macroeconomic stability.

— Sustainable use of scarce resources.

— Economic growth.

— Sustainable economic activities in environmental terms.

— Equitable distribution of economic activities in each region of the country.

— A balanced geographical distribution of the population.

— Equitable distribution of economic benefits.

— Maintaining a low and acceptable rate of inflation.

— Currency stability.

Tourism Development in Fiji

Tourism is Fiji's leading industry in terms of foreign exchange earnings and employment opportunities. Average room occupancies in Fiji are low. The national annual average is 53.9 per cent because tourism is a seasonal industry, with the peak season from June to November when tourists from the northern hemisphere go south to escape the chilling winter at home.

In late 1994, the government announced incentives aimed at encouraging more upmarket hotel development. This created a great deal of interest among investors and hotel operators. Prime hotel sites on Vulani Island and another major multi-property development project in Nadi are ready for sale, while many existing hotels and resorts have embarked on major refurbishment programmes.

Fiji is trying to complement the sun, sand and sea type of tourism, which is available at all competing holiday destinations. The new focus is on providing with a "Fiji visitors' experience" through its diverse cultures and beauty, and ecotourism. The aim is to offer seasoned Fiji visitors and newcomers other aspects of the nation, apart from its beaches and resorts.

These include a generally untouched landscape, unspoiled by logging or mining and a culture that is rich in exotic customs, crafts and events, with a variety of activities. The idea is to complement existing resorts by providing more attractions to entice tourists to experience Fiji.

Tourism is Fiji's largest gross foreign exchange earner. The industry employs some 40,000 people and is seen as offering the best opportunity for long-term growth compared to all other industries. Tourism provides Fiji with many benefits. Statistics show it contributes about $F 65 a week on average for every family in Fiji.

In 1998, the industry earned $F 568.2 million in foreign exchange for Fiji. This was more than sugar and other major industry such as garments, gold, fisheries and timber. In Fiji, tourism is largely a private sector activity. However, due to its contribution to the economy, government recognizes that it also has a critical role to play in providing infrastructure and marketing support for the industry.

Great success in tourism development has been achieved when government and the private sector have worked in close partnership. With full government backing, tourism is poised to become Fiji's largest industry in the near future. It is now at a turning point. Fiji has some accommodation facilities that are of world standard. These include the upmarket hideaway resorts along the Coral Coast, island resorts and cruises.

Compared to competing destinations, there are relatively few international hotel management groups operating in Fiji. Although there has been some investment in new resorts and refurbishment, these projects have tended to be relatively modest in size. In the past decade, no major hotels and resorts have been built in Fiji. The largest number of rooms is in the Nadi area, followed by the Coral Coast.

A broad range of incentives and concessions are provided in order to facilitate tourism investment activities including:

— Hotels Aid Investment Allowance

— Accelerated Depreciation Allowance

— Hotels Aid Act

— Carry forward of losses.99

— Work permits

— Duty concessions

Hotels Aid Act

Approved hotel construction or expansion projects may be entitled to an investment allowance under the Hotels Aid Act. The allowance lets a hotel owner to set 55 per cent of the approved capital expenditure (less the cost of land) against chargeable income arising from the hotel or extension until claimed in full.

The tax amendment provides that where it has not been possible to fully use the investment allowance against profits derived from the hotel or extension within five years following the year in which the hotel extension was completed, the balance can be used as profits for any other hotel operated by the taxpayer.

Hoteliers may also claim depreciation allowance on the full capital expenditure for buildings and equipment when they opt for the 55 per cent investment allowance. In the case of ownership, any unused concession or incentives may be carried forward to the new owner, subject to the approval of the Minister of Tourism, upon the advice of the Solicitor-General.

This means that there is a reduction in the taxable income of the investors concerned as well as consolidation of the investors' working capital position, which will enhance both current and future operational capabilities of the company. The Ministry of Tourism is responsible for administering assistance under the Hotels Aid Act and all applications for this concession/ incentives must be made to the Minister.

To obtain the benefits of the provisions of the Hotels Aid Act, an application in writing needs to be made to the Ministry of Tourism, using guidelines set out in the Act, with incentive awards being approved by the Minister responsible for tourism in a two-stage process involving: (a) preliminary approval and (b) final approval.

A crucial element should be the design of hotels and resorts, which should reflect Fijian themes in order to meet the desire of visitors for a distinctive destination with its own culture and traditions.

The location of tourism facilities in Fiji has often been driven by the availability of freehold land. This has resulted in a lack of resort centers. Such centers generally have a cluster of hotels and other tourist facilities including a marina, shops, sporting facilities, restaurants and entertainment. A resort center enables tourists to enjoy a range of different facilities.

In Fiji, many individual hotels, resort properties, and indeed whole islands, produce an excellent product and have a loyal and growing market in specialist segments. There is no doubt that Fiji is missing out on the major parts of the market, which wants the more comprehensive and active facilities found at resort centers.

The Town Planning Act (1978) is the legal basis for the planning and control of development. Under the Act, the general provisions of 1980 provide the detailed basis for standards for town planning schemes and areas. Provision 9, Schedule C of the general provisions covers hotels, tourist apartments, private hotels, boarding houses and guesthouses.

There are a number of separate building rules and regulations for hotels. A draft National Building Code covers structure, fire resistance and liability, provision for escape, access for disabled persons, health and amenities, and other factors. Adequate fire regulations are of particular importance in tourism, given the liability that overseas tour operators now have to cover for misadventures of their clients.

In general, the Department of Town and Country Planning requires a 30-metre setback from the high water mark for all coastal development. This somewhat inhibits over water development for tourism, which has become popular elsewhere in Asia and the Pacific. However, the government has agreed in principle that it will grant foreshore leases for such developments.

All tourist establishments should have adequate and sustainable water supplies in terms of quality and quantity, in relation to the type and scale of development. Drainage should be adequate to prevent dampers and damage. Building levels should take into account storm surge. Hygienic collection and storage facilities should be provided, preferably with separation for recycling.

Fiji enjoys a tropical climate that allows the production of a wide range of foodstuffs, both for local consumption and export, and provides one of the basic attractions for the tourist industry. The generally benign climate of Fiji is, however, punctuated by climate extremes in the form of hurricanes, floods and drought.

These extremes of climate have serious economic, social and environmental consequences that require prudent macroeconomic management, proper land use, planning, and water and watershed management.

Fiji is irrevocably becoming part of a world economy that is moving towards freer trade. The framework of rules within which economic activity takes place is defined by international organizations such as the World Trade Organization (WTO). The process of globalization presents both challenges and opportunities for a small country. Fiji became a member of WTO in 1996 and has since been accorded most-favoured-nation tariff levels.

The increasing integration of the world economy also means that Fiji is no longer immune to negative international developments, such as the recent Asian economic crisis. Electricity and telecommunication prices are relatively high due to the lack of competition, as well as inefficiencies in public enterprises providing these services. In contrast, water and sewerage charges are highly subsidized, and the costs of providing these services are expensive for the government to maintain.

As 99 per cent of international tourists arrive in Fiji by air, adequate and appropriate air services must be in place to meet demand. Advantage should be taken of changes in the international aviation environment, such as increased liberalization, frequency of charter flights and new aircraft. Internally, air access to all parts of Fiji is still somewhat limited and relatively expensive, and dispersal of visitors across the country remains at a low-level.

Changing consumer demand for a unique and individual holiday experience is driving the need for the continuing development of new tourism products. These products must be matched to the holiday needs of visitors and add depth to the overall image of Fiji. It will therefore be necessary to provide a wide range of facilities and infrastructure that cater to the future needs of international visitors. This includes accommodation, air access, airport facilities and transportation infrastructure.

New Opportunities of Tourism in Indonesia

Indonesia is the world's largest archipelago with 17,508 islands. If the map of Indonesia is placed on the map of Europe, Sabang of Sumatra will be on London and Merauke of Irian Jaya will cover Ankara. The country possesses incomparable tourism assets, including natural beauty, originality, scarcity, wholesomeness, richness of culture, flora and fauna, ecosystems and natural phenomena.

National tourism development in Indonesia is geared towards tourism becoming a mainstay of the economy, capable of stimulating economic activities including those in related sectors. Tourism will thereby create more jobs, contribute towards higher incomes, and increase national, provincial and local revenue. Increases in state revenue and foreign exchange earnings will result from efforts to develop and wisely use the national potential for tourism.

The core aim of national tourism development is to enhance the material and spiritual well being of people in a secure, orderly and peaceful atmosphere. In the international context, its aim is to promote freedom, brotherhood and peace. The broad outline for national tourism development is:

— To expand employment opportunities and ensure their more equitable distribution.

— To raise national income in order to enhance the welfare of the people and increase their prosperity.

— To foster a love of Indonesia and strengthen international friendship.

Between 1982 and 1997, the number of foreign visitors to Indonesia increased from 5,900 to 5.1 million. In 1998, due to political and economic circumstances, the number of foreign visitors declined to 4.6 million. That decrease was the first in two decades. In 1998, holiday tourists accounted for 51.77 per cent of the total arrivals, while business visitors amounted to a 46.46 per cent. This compares to 1997, when business visitors took first place followed by holiday tourists.

In 1999, successful political reform occurred in Indonesia, with a peaceful democratic national election in June and the election of a new Parliament. Other important indicators that show Indonesia is progressing, include a stabilized currency, reduced inflation and interest rates, the implementation of successful debt restructuring, and general improvements in trade and commerce.

The government has established a tourism strategy in recognition of the impressive potential of the industry to contribute to national development. One of the key approaches to developing the travel industry in Indonesia is to further encourage community-based tourism, as one of the most valuable national assets is our people.

Indonesian tourism is enriched by the cultural diversity of more than 300 distinct ethnic groups, each showing a uniqueness in life rituals and expression. This fascinating diversity has become a major attraction in the Indonesian tourism experience, and one that is being carefully protected. With an abundance of natural resources, Indonesia gives special attention to environmental conservation.

Located on the equator, Indonesia has some of richest biodiversity in the world, which must be carefully maintained for future generations. Focus is placed on product diversification at locations throughout the country. Through government support, emphasis is being given to "going eastward" in the archipelago, with further development and the promotion of unique marine and cultural-based tourism opportunities.

Among other projects, the private sector has developed several new tourist resorts around the country. Emphasis is also being put on market diversification through better professional communication about tourism potential. Any one of several major travel destinations can satisfy the interests of many types of markets, including different age levels.

Based on a study conducted by the World Travel and Tourism Council (WTTC) in Indonesia, in 1997, travel and tourism were expected to produce Rp 64,480 billion ($US 26 billion) in gross output and 6.6 million jobs, representing 8.6 per cent and 4 per cent of annual real growth, respectively, from 1998. By 2007, travel and tourism in Indonesia are projected to total Rp 248,363 billion ($US 67 billion) in gross output and 8.5 million jobs.

Indonesian travel and tourism was expected to produce 9.1 per cent of the gross domestic product (GDP) in 1997. By 2007, this contribution is projected to increase to 10.1 per cent. Between 1997 and 2007, gross output from travel and tourism is expected to increase by 113 per cent in real terms, or an average of 7.8 per cent annually. In Indonesia, employment resulting from travel and tourism was expected to total 8 per cent in 1997, or one in every 12.6 jobs. By 2007, this figure is expected to grow to 8.8 per cent in every 11.4 jobs.

Indirect taxes from travel and tourism in 1997 were expected to total Rp 2,712 billion or 8.7 per cent of total indirect taxes, while it expected to earn Rp 4,294 billion, or 9.4 per cent of total of government operating expenditures. Over the next decade, indirect taxes are expected to grow to Rp 10,580 billion, while government spending is expected to rise to Rp 10,511 billion.

Most areas of the Indonesian economy, including the tourism sector, are now open to foreign investment, with the exception of those on the prohibited list, which includes the retail trade and support services. A foreign investment company or Penanaman Modal Asing (PMA) is regulated under the Foreign Investment Law of 1967 and must be incorporated under the Indonesian Corporate Law as a Perseroan Terbatas (PT) or a limited liability company.

The operating permit granted to a PMA company is valid for 30 years from incorporation and can be extended for a further 30 years. The Act was improved in 1970. According to government regulation No. 20/1995, there is no required minimum amount of investment. The amount is determined on the basis of the scale of business and other commercial considerations. It is also subject to approval by BKPM, the government agency responsible for evaluating investment proposals and granting approval for foreign investment.

Government initiatives to promote investment included:

— Tax free imports of 100 per cent for machinery/primary equipment.

— A 50 per cent tax reduction for imports of machinery/primary equipment.

— Postponement of VAT payments on imports of machinery/equipment.

Currently, 56 areas in eastern Indonesia have been identified as priority areas. Considering the limited budget available, of those 56 priority areas, 13 have been selected as Integrated Economic Development Zones (KAPET). The Indonesian economy experienced a deep cyclical swing during the past five years, ranging from high growth to deep recession.

By the time the region's economic crisis erupted in the second half of 1997, the GDP growth rate in Indonesia had already fallen by 50 per cent from its peak level. The economic crisis transformed a soft landing into a deep recession. Economic activity shrank in the first half of 1998 with a decline in the annual GDP rate of about 12 per cent. A decline of 10-15 per cent in GDP had been projected for 1998 as a whole.

The manufacturing sector was the main engine of growth from 1994 to 1996, with an average annual growth rate of 12 per cent, slightly above the average of 10 per cent in the previous decade. The period was also characterized by the rapid growth of the service sector, including tourism, which now accounts for 40 per cent of total output.

Since mid-1997, however, production has been on the decline in all sectors. Economic activity from 1994 to 1996 was driven by high levels of investment, some of which was domestic and foreign investment in the tourism sector, and to a lesser extent by exports. On the other hand, the flourishing economic activity was also marked by a rapid rise in private consumption that included, among other things, travel services.

This was a relatively new factor in Indonesia's development process and was linked to the considerable increase in living standards and private borrowing. Since the second half of 1997, however, domestic demand has been strongly affected by a drop in investment, the decline of the banking and corporate sectors, and a decrease in personal income. Prudent fiscal and monetary policies have been a major factor in Indonesia's long economic expansion.

The country entered the economic crisis with relatively sound macroeconomic fundamentals, i.e., a balanced budget, an inflation rate below 10 per cent and an increasing but sustainable current account deficit. However, the fall of the rupiah against the US dollar caused a deterioration in macroeconomic performance as evidenced by the sharp rise in domestic inflation, the increase in the cost of imports to prohibitive levels, and the situation of insolvency that has impaired the financing of production and trade.

In the early weeks of the regional economic crisis, Indonesia appeared to be relatively less affected than most of its neighbours. Recent surveys have shown that market sentiment about Indonesia, still favourably influenced by past growth and macroeconomic performance, remained relatively positive until August 1997.

Tourism development facilities

The establishment and development of tourism facilities is not only aimed at meeting demand in terms of numbers but also at satisfying the needs for various types of facilities throughout Indonesia. However, even today, special facilities for tourists remain limited to the main tourist destinations such as Bali and some areas in Java.

Indonesia has a policy of closely coordinating the national transportation system, including the road system, railways and sea, river and air transportation. The overall transportation system is meant to support the success of all economic sectors, including the tourism sector, by providing tourism facilities with infrastructure. The policy of such a transportation policy is to ensure a smooth flow in the transportation of people and goods in support of national economic development.

Domestic tourism travel is mainly by land, using land transportation means that are also available for foreign tourists, mainly in Java and Bali. Land transportation is not only provided for tourists, but also for the benefit of the local people. Land transportation is also supported by a railway system. However, this facility is only available in Java and north, west and south Sumatra.

There are 600 harbours and seaports throughout Indonesia, of which 320 are maintained as public seaports. Some others are harbours for specific needs. The main harbours opened as international entry points for international tourists are Belawan in Medan, north Sumatra, Tanjung Priok in Jakarta, Tanjung Perak in Surabaya, east Java and Hasanudin in Makassar, south Sulawesi. Padangbai Harbour in Bali, Tanjung Priok in Jakarta and Tanjung Mas in Semarang are often visited by cruise ships.

Ferry transportation is used as a means of crossing some straits such as the Sunda and Bali Straits. The ferry points are directly connected with land transportation systems from Aceh to Kupang. As part of the effort to boost the economy, investment in the tourism industry is crucial. Various policies aimed at developing an attractive investment climate, simplifying investment procedures and providing smooth services have been implemented by the government.

Tourism development in Maldives

Tourism in Maldives began in the early 1970s with the arrival of some guests from Europe. Since then, tourism has grown to become the largest industry in the country and contributes up to 20 per cent of the gross domestic product (GDP), 70 per cent of total foreign exchange earnings and 40 per cent of total government revenue. In fact, the real magnitude of the contribution by tourism to the local economy is far greater than the above figures.

The growth of the tourism industry has led to rapid growth in support industries such as air transport, construction, distribution and retailing. In addition, the industry provides thousands of jobs for the local population who have enjoyed rising living standards over the past two decades.

The direction of the tourism industry in Maldives is guided by the Tourism Master Plan, the broad objectives of which are to:

— Extend the economic benefits of tourism to island populations located away from traditional tourism centers.

— Diversify the Maldives' tourism product.

— Diversify the income and job generating markets and reduce dependence on just a few markets.

— Emphasize human resource development with the aim of reducing dependence on foreign labour.

— Increase bed capacity to reach 20,000 beds by the end of the plan period.

— Develop complementary services, i.e., airport capacity and facilities, transfers, marketing, etc.

Government efforts to achieve the objectives identified in the current Tourism Master Plan have been reasonably successful, with many of the recommendations being implemented as the mid-term review of the plan approaches. Tourism in Maldives has undergone impressive changes since its inception in the early 1970s. The size of the industry has expanded, as have all the complementary industries.

The supply of resort facilities and demand for the Maldive tourism product has increased considerably over the past 28 years. In 1972, when tourism was first introduced, there were just two resort islands with a total bed capacity of 280 and an annual tourist arrival of 1,097. Today, there are over 80 resorts with a bed capacity in excess of 15,000, while annual tourist arrivals have surpassed the 400,000 mark.

Recent years has seen the expansion of the industry's bed capacity with the lease of 13 new islands for resort development under the first phase of the current Tourism Master Plan. The sudden increase in bed capacity has resulted in a drop in the national occupancy rate and has alarmed investors in the sector.

For many experienced entrepreneurs, the impact of the bed increase on the national occupancy rate is a temporary phenomenon that will soon be corrected by market forces. They argue that the industry is in a transition phase and that the same drop in occupancies was experienced during the previous round of bed increases. At present, there are 84 resorts with a total of 14,956 beds, 129 safari boats with bed capacity of 1,852 and seven hotels with a total bed capacity of 466.

When looking at the Maldive tourism product, it can be said that the traditional dive and beach holidays for which Maldives is well known are no longer the only attraction. The products offered include surfing, a wide range of land and water sports and, more importantly, the expanding cruise product that is already very popular. As far as generating markets are concerned, the dependence on a limited number of European markets is still strong.

However, efforts to diversify the markets, both by the government and the private sector, is paying off as the numbers of arrivals from other countries are on the rise. Maldives has also ventured into the Asian and North American markets and the results so far have been very impressive.

The economic benefits of tourism are clear, at least in the Maldivian context. Since the inception of tourism some 28 years ago, the country has enjoyed sustained GDP growth averaging 8-12 per cent accompanied by modest inflation, and the population has consistently enjoyed rising living standards. The industry has opened ample opportunities for the establishment and growth of support industries such as transportation, construction, distribution and retailing.

Several estimates suggest that the industry's contribution to the local economy is indeed very large. The industry accounts for over 40 per cent of government revenue through direct taxes and lease rents on islands. In addition, a significant share of the revenue that the government generates from import duties originates from the tourism sector.

That revenue from tourism is then utilized by the government for investment in social development and other community/infrastructure projects. Without tourism, government ability to spend on such programmes would be highly restricted. It is estimated that 70 per cent of foreign exchange inflows into the economy comes directly from tourism. For a country that is more or less dependent on imports, foreign exchange from tourism is crucial to financing the import bill.

Tourism also generates direct employment opportunities for the growing population of Maldives as well as indirect employment opportunities in complementary industries such as transportation, construction, distribution and retailing. However, the true potential of the sector has yet to be exploited. Due to various limitations that exist in the economy and society, a fairly substantial proportion of the tourism industry is still in the hands of foreigners.

Considering the local/foreign employment structure in the tourism sector, it is regrettable to note that over 40 per cent of the tourism workforce comprises expatriates. Due to this heavy dependence on expatriate labour, a substantial amount of tourism dollars are lost in the form of wage remittances. This situation needs to change if the real benefits of tourism for the economy are to be attained.

Another area of concern to the government is the proportion of foreign ownership in the industry. The situation is far from ideal, at least from the perspective of the government, since the returns on investments in the tourism industry are very attractive.

In general, tourism infrastructure is taken as encompassing the basic facilities such as transportation, communications, power supplies, buildings and human resources that enable the industry to function as an income-generating economic activity. When looking more closely at tourism infrastructure, two main types can be identified. First, there is the infrastructure that forms the building blocks of the industry such as the resorts and hotels. Second, and more important, is the so-called indirect infrastructure such as airports, airstrips, harbours, etc., which form the driving force behind the success of the industry.

For tourism to develop as it has in Maldives, it is crucial to have basic supporting infrastructure in place. If one looks back at the beginnings of tourism in Maldives, it is evident that infrastructure supportive of tourism growth was virtually non-existent at that time. Even travel experts who conducted feasibility studies for tourism development in Maldives ruled out tourism with the then-existing infrastructure despite the unique environment of the country.

However, since the inception of tourism in the early 1970s, the industry has boomed and investments in supporting infrastructure have materialized. Maldives' tourism is unique in many ways. Resorts, the primary tourist facility in the Maldivian context, are self-contained units that include all the necessary infrastructure for operations, such as electricity, water and gas.

Investments in resort development therefore take into account all these costs, which is the primary reason for the relatively large investments in resort development and the portrayal of Maldives as an expensive destination. In addition to the above infrastructure, there is obviously a need to invest in infrastructure that enables clients to reach their holiday destination as well as in human capital, which is considered vital to the success of the industry.

These investments include expanding the existing airport, the establishment of new airports, airstrips and resort service centers, and human resource development. For any tourism activity to be successful, it is critical that the destination has easy and convenient international accessibility. Maldives experienced its initial years of tourism with a relatively underdeveloped airport that had very basic facilities.

The government, having realized the importance of an international airport, gave top priority on its infrastructure development agenda to upgrading the airport. As a result, the current small, yet modern, airport in Maldives is the direct result of that government initiative. With the ever-increasing number of visitor arrivals, the need to expand the present runway and other airport facilities has once again taken center stage in the government's capital investment agenda.

In addition to upgrading efforts directed at Male International Airport, the need to invest in the development of four regional airports currently utilized for domestic transfers is becoming increasingly urgent. With the spread of tourism to the outer atolls, the issue of transferring guests to the resorts is becoming increasingly difficult.

The government has taken the lead role in promoting investments in infrastructure, and it has made considerable inroads in establishing airports, airstrips, harbours, jetties, etc. Obviously, the finance for those investments in tourism infrastructure is generated from various sources. Once again, a considerable share of the investments comes from the government budget, which in turn is financed from revenue generated by the tourism sector.

The increasing importance of cruise tourism has prompted the government to explore the feasibility of a yacht marina in Maldives. This new initiative has taken shape with a decision to tender out the development of a marina in the north of the country. This new initiative is consistent with the goals of the government to diversify the Maldive tourism product, and it is expected that this initial development will be emulated in several other locations in the Maldives.

The existing infrastructure is facing supply-side bottlenecks in the ever-increasing number of tourist arrivals. With an average arrival growth at 10-12 per cent per annum, the present international airport can barely cope with passenger traffic. Tourism is a service-driven industry, and in today's competitive environment the need for trained professionals who can deliver world-class service has become crucial.

Human resource development has been identified as a key concern, and the need to invest in human capacity-building has been long recognized by the government. However, it is disappointing to note that the expected commitment from the private sector on human resource development issues has not been forthcoming. With over 40 per cent of total employment in the tourism sector being taken up by foreigners, the economic and social cost to the nation can easily run into millions in monetary terms.

While some might consider human resources development to be outside the domain of tourism infrastructure, the issue is a key concern of the government and needs significant investment in order to change the current situation.

At present, visitors arriving in Maldives are transferred to their respective resorts by either speedboat or seaplane. With the projected expansion of tourism to the outer atolls, the need for a more reliable transfer system will become a priority issue. The development of resorts at great distances from the airport also raises the question of supplying the resorts with day-to-day raw materials such as fruit, vegetables and other consumer requirements.

Under current conditions, resort supplies are transferred by boat, which is time consuming and expensive. Obviously, the need to invest in airstrips has been recognized and some private sector applications to develop airstrips have already been submitted to the government. Investments in this area, for example, would diversify the resort transfer mechanism currently in place and would give the consumers greater choice.

In view of the importance and heavy reliance of the economy on tourism, the move to invest in tourism infrastructure has always received top priority. However, the expected private sector response to investments in tourism infrastructure has not been forthcoming due to various reasons. The attractiveness of investing in resorts far outweighs the returns from investments in tourism-related infrastructure investments. Hence, the willingness of the private sector to invest in infrastructure development other than development of resorts is limited and the government has always had to take the initiative in tourism infrastructure development.

Tourism Development in Mynmar

Tourism has become a growth sector in the national economy following the liberalization of policies under the current market-oriented economy. The Myanmar Tourism Law of 1990, which was revised in 1993, was promulgated to enable the systematic development of the hotel and tourism industry; it encourages active private sector participation in the tourism industry.

Over the past 10 years, there has been significant growth in visitor arrivals as a result of liberalized policies and promotion. Visitor arrivals rose rapidly from 60,000 in 1993/94 to nearly 200,000 in 1999/2000. The growth slowed between 1997 and 1999 due to the economic crisis in the Asian region. Total visitor arrivals for the year

2000 were projected at 240,000, representing 20 per cent growth rate.

Visitor arrival categories include tourists, business travelers, and Myanmar expatriates visiting friends and relatives (10 per cent). Among the tourists, independent travelers account for 47 per cent and packaged tours for 22 per cent. By nationality, the Japanese top the list at 18 per cent, followed by Taiwanese, French (9 per cent), Singaporeans, Americans, Germans, British and Italians.

The government has recognized the tourism industry as a major source of foreign exchange earnings and employment opportunities for the local community. Tourism income for the country is quite substantial, but most of the income is earned mainly by the private sector. The revenue from tourism revolves through the local community. Employment, both direct and indirect, created by tourism is substantial.

The construction and operating of hotels, restaurants, souvenir shops, transport services and other tourism-related businesses are the main sources of employment in the tourism industry. On the other hand, Myanmar is quite cautious about the potentially negative impact of tourism on social and cultural values.

Although Myanmar has abundant tourist attractions, infrastructure remains a major constraint to rapid tourism development. To overcome the problem, the government has rushed through many projects in order to improve existing facilities and provide new infrastructure facilities. However, the government's efforts have been seriously constrained by the lack of offshore funds from international institutions such as the World Bank and Asian Development Bank (ADB).

Myanmar, therefore, has diverse attractions and is an ideal place for investors who are interested in property and estate development. In addition to tourism-related investment, a sound infrastructure (airports, roads, railways, telecommunication, etc.) is crucial for the promotion of tourism, and investors seeking opportunities in these areas are welcomed. Myanmar still needs to improve its infrastructure, mainly in the energy, communications, and transport sectors.

Myanmar can offer many cultural attractions, scenic views and natural unspoiled beauty, different ethnic groups, and traditional arts and crafts throughout the country. Myanmar can offer many unspoiled, natural areas, which is a resource that most countries now lack, and which most tourists are seeking. However, accessibility to such areas remains a constraint due to the lack of adequate infrastructure.

Tourism Development in Nepal

Although tourism is considered to be major component of the Nepalese economy, tourism development in Nepal has, so far, been concentrated in a few major locations and confined to a few major products. While cultural tourism is centred in and around the capital, Kathmandu, and the town of Pokhara, trekking is popular in the Khumbu, Langtang, and Annapurna regions. Chitwan is the focus of wildlife tourism.

The current Tourism Policy of 1996 has given good encouragement to the private sector in tourism development. The envisaged role of the private sector relates to tourism diversification, while the government's role will be to develop the infrastructure needed for tourism development. The private sector will be required to maintain certain standards for the provision of facilities and services, and to encourage the adoption of codes of conduct.

The tourism policy identifies the lines of responsibility between the Tourism Council (issuing general guidelines), Ministry of Tourism and Civil Aviation (policy and regulatory matters) and the Nepal Tourism Board (policy implementation, including tourism planning, product development, marketing and promotion). Tourism has been growing as the leading sector earning foreign currency over the years. Tourism contributed about 4.4 per cent to the gross domestic product (GDP) of Nepal during the Eighth Development Plan.

An important aspect of tourism is its employment-generating potential. Tourism in Nepal has not only been providing employment for the educated and trained elite, but also for poor and underprivileged people in remote areas of the country through adventure activities. In mountain areas, people are finding employment opportunities through tourism. The living standards of people in areas with tourism activity is far better than those of their counterparts in areas where there is no tourism.

Tourism has acted as a tool to promote these items and has given such products much needed international exposure. There are basically four sources of funding for infrastructure investment:

(a) the public sector with funds raised through taxation or domestic borrowing;

(b) local entrepreneurs using their own funds and/or loans;

(c) foreign investors; and

(d) aid donors.

Both the central government and the civic authorities have provisions for charging such tax, which is ultimately used to fund various infrastructure investments. The private sector performs the role of a service provider and is basically confined to a variety of tourism services such as travel transport, trekking and rafting agencies, restaurants, etc.

Various donor agencies are the ultimate investors in infrastructure. About 15 agencies have been supporting projects that have directly or indirectly contributed to tourism development across the country. Australia, Canada, France, Germany, Japan and the United Kingdom have provided significant assistance to the civil aviation subsector, mainly in the form of grants.

Agencies such as the United Nations Development Programme (UNDP) and the International Civil Aviation Organization (ICAO) have supplemented bilateral efforts to strengthen the Royal Nepalese Airlines Corporation and other aviation sector institutions. The Asian Development Bank (ADB) has also extended technical and financial assistance to various tourism development programmes.

Industries that build and operate roads, bridges, tunnels, ropeways, flying bridges, trolleybuses and trams have received national priority. In order to attract more foreign investment, various policy measures have been implemented, including the streamlining of the administrative machinery, trade liberalization, tariff rationalization, tax reform, and financial sector reform with full convertibility of Nepalese rupees (NRs) in current accounts.

Foreign investors and who want to invest in 100 per cent ownership with assets up to NRs 500 million can apply directly to the Department of Industry, which can grant permission after a detailed evaluation. However, investments exceeding NRs 500 million in fixed assets are allowed upon the approval of the Industrial Promotion Board.

Tourism Development in Pakistan

Pakistan is a country of contrasts ranging from tropical areas to snow-capped mountains. It is vast, varied and strikingly beautiful. As a tourist attraction it has almost everything required. Most of all, apart from the abundant natural beauty, Pakistan presents a major challenge to any lover of history, archaeology and ancient civilization.

The oldest architectural remains are those of the cities of Mohenjodaro and Harappa, dating from 3000 to 2500 B.C. Spectacular mountain ranges and towering peaks can be found that offer unequalled opportunities for trekking and mountaineering, while the country's forests and lakes are a delight for bird watchers and nature lovers. Tourism in Pakistan, as it is today, has been shaped by history, land, economy and socio-cultural traditions.

During 1998, Pakistan hosted 430,000 tourists, which was an increase of 14.4 per cent over the 370,000 tourist arrivals in 1997. The current position in Pakistan, however, is not enviable. Since 1971, the year in which tourist statistics were first compiled, tourist arrivals have registered between 122,000 and 500,000. The growth of tourism in Pakistan has remained uneven, influenced by economic and political developments at the national and international levels, thus revealing the high volatility of international tourism.

With a current per capita income of US$ 450, Pakistan today is no longer among the poorest countries in the world. Despite this fact, many socio-economic features in Pakistan are similar to the rest of the third world. One of the common features is an adverse balance of payments. Pakistan's economy is still predominantly agrarian.

More then half of the population is not able to read and write. However, the government and people of Pakistan are determined to overcome economic problems in the shortest possible time and at minimum resource costs.

Tourism has special significance for developing countries that possess attractions of tourist merit. Like many other industries, it offers numerous economic benefits. The development of tourism results in the distribution of income among various income groups, and it benefits less developed regions. Tourism in Pakistan ranks one of the top 10 foreign exchange earning industries.

Due to lack of investment in product development, promotion and marketing, the potential of tourism in Pakistan has remained largely unknown in the tourist generating countries of Western Europe, North America and the East and South-East Asia.

Foreign investment flows into Pakistan has also remained severely restricted due to the lack of tourist infrastructure in the northern areas, the North West Frontier Province and other areas of tourist merit. Management steps to create an institutional framework to deal with investment have not been taken. Tourism projects were eligible for a small revolving credit line sanctioned by the country's central bank (the State Bank of Pakistan) in the early 1990s and administered by the Regional Development Finance Corporation (RDFC).

However, that source of funds has since been withdrawn. Although the National Tourism Policy provided a number of fiscal and monetary incentives for investors, most of the monetary benefits have either been withdrawn or the private sector has not been able to utilize them due to bureaucratic difficulties. Some of the tourism-specific investment incentives offered in Pakistan are:

Tourism has been declared as a service industry and the private sector no longer requires NOC for setting up tourism projects. Equity participation is allowed for loans intended for the establishment of tourism projects, and full repatriation of profits from tourism projects is allowed. The government has waived work permit restrictions on the employment of foreign nationals in the category of general managers and technical personnel in the hotel sector.

In various parts of the country, 170 plots of government land have been earmarked for investors in tourism projects on soft terms. Under the "free sky" policy, private airline companies are allowed to operate on domestic/foreign routes. In addition, helicopter services have also been allowed to undertake commercial operation for the promotion of tourism within the country.

Despite many shortcomings and a lukewarm attitude towards the development of tourism, the government through the Pakistan Tourism Development

Corporation (PTDC) invested PRs 445,682 million in the development of tourism between 1990 and 1998. PTDC, which is the commercial wing of the Ministry of Culture, Sports, Tourism and Youth Affairs, has completed 18 motels with a total of 227 rooms while another 10 motels are in various stages of completion in various areas.

The development and provision of infrastructure, such as roads, bridges, airports, electricity supplies and sewerage disposal, is essentially the responsibility of the government, whereas the development of tourist-oriented infra- and supra-structure is an activity of both the public and private sectors. Planned development of infrastructure is a prerequisite for sustainable development of tourism that does not harm the original character, attractiveness and the natural, archaeological or historical appeal of the tourism asset.

Investment in tourist-oriented infrastructure should be planned and integrated. Infrastructure is simply a means of making places of tourist attraction accessible and enjoyable. While making investment in tourist infrastructure, it should not be forgotten that the beneficiaries of these facilities are not only local and foreign tourists. Certain facilities such as roads and electricity supplies will also benefit local communities. Therefore, the size and quality of investment should be compatible with the estimated number of tourists and general public multiplied by the projected revenue from the tourist and other socio-economic benefits.

The present status of tourism in Pakistan shows that that immediate investment is required for developing tourist facilities that cater to the spatial, accommodation, comfort and safety needs of tourists, while also meeting socio-environmental norms. In a country with limited financial and entrepreneurial resources, tourism competes with other sectors such as defence, education, agriculture, health and industry. The low-priority sectors such as tourism have largely remained ignored since the creation of Pakistan.

The low level of public sector investment in tourism is attributable to the low government priority attached to tourism. The size and variety of private sector investment in tourism is also not enviable. There are various reasons for the poor private sector response to tourism. Investment in tourism, as in any other business activity, is a function of potential return on capital attractiveness of gestation/breakeven period, and profitability and growth potential.

Unstable government investment policies, the high seasonality indices of tourism, the lack of basic infrastructure, an absence of marketing and awareness, the social predisposition against certain forms of tourism, the shortage of potable water and supplies of electricity, poor access roads in and around tourist areas, poor and impracticable air links, the lack of business intuition and the very high guaranteed returns on government savings schemes are cited as main reasons negatively influencing investment decisions in tourism in Pakistan.

In a less developed country such as Pakistan, the demands and expectations of the private sector are gradually rising. In addition to umbrella marketing of the country and the provision of infrastructure, the government is expected to offer attractive fiscal and monetary incentives and concessions for the tourism industry. However, the resource-short government finds it difficult to meet much requirements.

In order to promote investment in tourism along scientific and professional lines, a comprehensive mission statement, clear objectives, and investment strategies and guidelines need to be outlined. More importantly, the financial and operational risks as perceived by potential local and foreign investors need to be addressed.

Tourism should be developed on a self-reliant basis, and where private sector investment is not forthcoming, the government could play a catalytic role. The government should establish a Tourism Investment Fund for providing concessions, incentives and wherever else is necessary.

4

Tourism and Rural Development Strategies

For many years a number of rural areas have been beset by population loss and declining services. These problems are now exacerbated by changes that have brought job losses and falling income to the farm sector. In contrast to this downturn, tourism has blossomed into a prosperous, fast-growing activity, and has indeed turned out to be a significant factor for economic growth in the countries in which it has developed.

It was therefore important to determine whether tourism's growth potential could be harnessed as a strategy for rural development, in particular by drawing upon resurgent interest in the countryside, its traditional way of life, and landscapes and the architectural heritage, referred to as amenities.

Relationship Between Rural Tourism and Agriculture

Across the rural regions of the developed world the

issues of population decline, economic change and community regeneration are universal. For over a century, the powerful trends of industrialisation and urbanisation have steadily altered the economic and political position of rural society. In the last 40 years those trends have intensified. Farm incomes have fallen in real terms.

Technological changes have joined with falling incomes to reduce agricultural employment. In response, rural service p ovision has diminished: shops, schools, churches, professional services and transport facilities have all declined in numbers and in underlying vitality. Typically, rural populations have aged and become fewer in total.

Many small towns and villages now struggle to retain their viability. Throughout the world, local, regional and central government agencies have intervened to address these issues, with various degrees of success. In recent years, the rural world has seen new challenges. Nature and landscape conservation is increasingly regarded as important.

Historic buildings and "traditional" rural societies are receiving more attention. In some more accessible rural regions, there has been an influx of population, of people unhappy about big city living conditions-a trend known as counter-urbanisation. But for most parts of the countryside, rural decline issues remain important.

Tourism on the contrary, presents a picture of thriving growth. From humble origins in the nineteenth century, tourism has expanded rapidly since the early 1950's. International tourist arrivals have increased from 25 millions in 1950 to an estimated 476 millions in 1992. About 60 per cent of this travel is for leisure purposes.

Domestic (non-international) tourism, however, dwarfs even these massive figures. The World Tourism Organization estimates domestic travel numbers to be ten times the international total. Domestic tourism is also growing rapidly. The WTO estimates that, by 2000, tourism could be the world's largest single industry.

There are many factors behind the growth statistics. In the developed world, there has been a rapid growth in disposable income. In Britain whose economic growth in recent years has not been very strong disposable income rose by 63 per cent in real terms between 1968 and 1988. Shorter working hours and increasing numbers of paid holidays have helped.

Higher levels of education have prompted a greater desire to travel, and explore. Transport networks rail, road, air and sea-have been greatly improved. Rarely, however, have government agencies directly influenced the pace of tourism development, which has largely been driven by market forces and private enterprise. In this way, tourism differs markedly from agriculture and other rural activities.

Tourism has, until recently, been concentrated into specialist beach, lake and mountain resort areas, and into major cultural centres. It has proved to be a powerful engine for economic growth-transferring capital, income and employment from industrial, urban and developed areas to non-industrial regions. Intra OECD tourism flows dominate the world pattern.

The top five tourist generating countries-Germany, United States, United Kingdom, Japan and France-account for over 51 per cent of world travel expenditure. Income flows are remarkably similar: the top five destination countries, accounting for 41 per cent of receipts, are the United States, Spain, Italy, France and the United Kingdom. Within that picture there have been real changes in the post war period. Foremost amongst the new destinations is Spain.

Foreign visitors to Spain increased from 6 millions in 1960 to 47 millions in 1986. Foreign earnings more than doubled—(to 15 billion US dollars)— between 1983 and 1987 alone. Tourism now employs over 1.5 million Spanish people directly. Yet the vast majority of Spain's visitors are concentrated into the five coastal regions of Spain, out of the total of 16 Spanish regions.

While the Spanish example illustrates how tourism can assist national economic growth, the experience of many other countries, including Britain, Ireland, France and the United States illustrates how regional economic growth can also be linked to tourism development.

Already tourism to rural regions is increasing. Rural tourism is not totally new. Interest in countryside recreation grew in the nineteenth century as a reaction to the stress and squalor of the expanding industrial cities. Writers such as Wordsworth and Schiller captured the romanticism of the rural scene.

The new railway companies capitalised on this emergent interest by transporting tourists to the countryside. The Alps and the American and Canadian Rockies were early rural tourism venues assisted by rail-led marketing and capital investment.

The new rural tourism of the 1970's, 80's and 90's is, however, different in several ways. Far larger numbers of visitors are involved. Over 70 per cent of all Americans now participate in rural recreation: figures for many other OECD countries reveal similar, if slightly lower, levels of participation. The penetration of those visitors is far greater. The spread of car ownership and internationally available car hire allows visitors to reach regions far beyond rail-nets and rail-heads.

Most important of all, tourism has developed away from spectacularly scenic areas into countryside of all types. It has also broken free of large and specialised resorts into small towns and villages to become truly rural. Growth in rural tourism is difficult to quantify, because few countries collect statistics in a way which separates purely rural from other forms of tourism. Most national tourism administrations agree, however, that it is a growth sector. Experience in individual rural regions provides further testimony.

In the American states of Wyoming, Montana and Idaho ranch and farm hospitality enterprises have increased from five in 1985 to 90 in 1992. Australia's "Outback Queensland" area reports steady annual increases in visitor flows of up to 20 per cent p.a. Many new tourism projects in rural Austria have achieved a steady development in patronage throughout the 1980's.

Rural tourism is tourism which takes place in the countryside. But, on deeper consideration, a simple definition of rural tourism is inadequate for many purposes. Equally, it is difficult to produce a more complex definition which applies to all rural areas in all countries. Problems include:

— Urban-or-resort-based tourism is not confined to urban areas, but spills out into rural areas;

— Rural areas themselves are difficult to define, and the criteria used by different nations vary enormously;

— it can be "urban" in form, and merely be located in a rural area;

— Tourism has historically been an urban concept; the great majority of tourists live in urban areas. Tourism can be an urbanising influence on rural areas, encouraging cultural and economic change, and new construction;

— Different forms of rural tourism have developed in different regions.

Rural areas themselves are in a complex process of change. The impact of global markets, communications and telecommunication have changed market conditions and orientations for traditional products. The rise of environmentalism has led to increasing control by "outsiders" over land use and resource development.

Although some rural areas still experience depopulation, others are experiencing an inflow of people to retire or to develop new "non-traditional" businesses. The once clear distinction between urban and rural is now blurred by suburbanisation, long distance commuting and second home development.

Rural tourism is a complex multifaceted activity: it is not just farm-based tourism. It includes farm-based holidays but also comprises special interest nature holidays and ecotourism, walking, climbing and riding holidays, adventure, sport and health tourism, hunting and angling, educational travel, arts and heritage tourism, and, in some areas, ethnic tourism.

There is also a large general interest market for less specialised forms of rural tourism. This area is highlighted by studies of the important German tourism market, where a major requirement of the main holiday is the ability to provide peace, quiet and relaxation in rural surroundings.

Because rural tourism is multifaceted, because rural areas themselves are multifaceted and rarely either static entities or self-contained, and free from urban influence, a working and reasonably universal definition of the subject is difficult to find. However, in almost every case rurality is the central and unique selling point in the rural tourism package. The search for a definition must, therefore, begin with an understanding of the concept of rurality itself.

The need for a definition of rural tourism is relatively new. The need for a definition for rurality in general is an old issue faced by geographers, sociologists, economists and planners for many years. Typically rural areas have low population densities: this is a result of small settlements, widely spaced apart. The natural and/or the farmed/forested environment dominates the built environment.

Average rural population densities vary enormously between and within the OECD countries: an exact analysis would be valueless because of the varying sizes of the administrative units used for statistical purposes. The OECD Rural Development Programme uses a pragmatically based series of indicators: while at local level a population density of 150 persons per square kilometre is the preferred criterion, "at the regional level geographic units are grouped by the share of their population which is rural, into the following three types: predominantly rural, significantly rural (15-50 per cent) and predominantly urbanized regions".

From this array of varying definitions, two clear points stand out. Rural settlements may vary in size, but they are small, and always with a population of fewer than 10,000 inhabitants. They are almost always in areas of relatively low population density.

Many commentators define rural areas as those with less than 10-20 per cent of their land areas covered by the built environment. There are three important implications here. These areas will be dominated by agrarian and forest-based economic activities. They will be, to a large extent, repositories of the natural world and wildlife.

For the visitor, they will give an impression of space, and a traditional non-urban, non-industrial economy. Their economies will be strongly influenced by the market for farm and forest products. Although the labour force required for farming and forestry has declined rapidly in recent years, rural areas still show a strong bias towards jobs in the farm/forest sector.

Additionally, they usually exhibit low female activity rates outside the home because of the shortage of job opportunities for women in many rural areas. The rapid urbanisation of the nineteenth and twentieth centuries produced new social structures different from the "traditional" societies of the countryside.

The retention of older ways of life and thinking is important in retaining rural "character". It is this residual character which, combined with the scenic values and recreational opportunities of the countryside, attracts tourists from urban areas. It is difficult to define the exact characteristics of rural society.

There are great variations between countries and continents, and even within countries. The rural sociologists have struggled hard to identify the varying characteristics of rural societies. Rural communities can be assessed on a sliding scale with sparsely populated remote wilderness as one end of a polar typology. The other end of the scale can be represented by the so-called "world city", the ultimate expression of urbanisation.

Between these extremes lie a variety of situations, largely rural or largely urban, with a midpoint represented by the outermost edge of suburbia, a crossover point between poles, exhibiting characteristics of both rural and urban typology. An additional part of the "rurality" equation can be introduced here. The OECD's Rural Development Programme has developed a useful typology for assessing the economic geography of rural areas.

This divides the rural world into peripheral or remote regions, "intermediate" regions, which make up the majority of the rural land mass, and economically integrated rural regions, often close to large urban complexes. The peripheral regions are characterised by sparse populations, small scale often traditional enterprises, high servicing costs and economic poverty.

The economically integrated regions tend to have large farm units, a diversified economy, good services and relative affluence. The intermediate areas lie midway between these extremes. This typology can also fit the continuum concept: the three types of region are not sharply defined but blend into each other. The typology has important implications for both rural development and rural tourism which will be explained later.

The continuum concept copes not only with a variety of landscapes, life styles and demographic inheritance-but also with change. Settlements can move along the continuum, exhibiting change through time. Typically-but not always-the change tends to move districts and settlements towards the urban pole. In the OECD's economic typology, change is also common-and can also occur in either direction.

Thus, rural settlements may remain locationally rural while becoming functionally urban. Settlement size and population density may remain "rural", but economies may become non-agricultural, and society may display increasing numbers of urban characteristics. Different parts of rural society may display more or less urban characteristics.

Thus, while the global condition has become steadily more urban, most commentators have stressed the importance of retaining key differences between urbanisation and the rural realm. Forty years ago, in 1951, the British government set up a special commission to review the future of that most remote and most rural part of Britain, the crofting communities of the Highlands and Islands of Scotland.

After noting that crofting flew in the face of all modern agrarian practices, and required, even in 1951, massive levels of state subsidy, the Commission concluded that, "in the national interest, the maintenance of these communities is desirable, because they embody a free and independent way of life which, in a civilisation predominantly urban and industrial in character, is worth preserving for its own intrinsic value".

Government policies financially support both primary rural products and rural service provision in every OECD Member country. These financial policies are frequently backed by strong conservation policies, aimed at the retention of existing landscape areas, whole settlements, buildings and the natural world. Urban conservation policies also exist, but usually cover only fragments of cities and isolated special situations.

Rurality as a concept is connected with low population densities and open space, and with small scale settlements, generally of fewer than 10, 000 inhabitants. Land use is dominated by farming, forestry and natural areas. Societies tend towards traditionalism: the influence of the past is often strong. Government policies lean towards conservation rather than radical or rapid change. It follows, therefore, that rural tourism should be:

— Located in rural areas;

— Functionally rural, built upon the rural world's special features: small scale enterprise, open space, contact with nature and the natural world, heritage, "traditional" societies and "traditional" practices;

— Rural in scale-both in terms of buildings and settlements-and, therefore, usually small scale;

— Traditional in character, growing slowly and organically, and connected with local families. It will often be very largely controlled locally and developed for the long term good of the area;

— Sustainable-in the sense that its development should help sustain the special rural character of an area, and in the sense that its development should be sustainable in its use of resources. Rural tourism should be seen as a potential tool for conservation and sustainability, rather than as an urbanizing and development tool;

— Of many different kinds, representing the complex pattern of rural environment, economy, and history.

A list of contrasting features between urban/resort tourism and rural tourism could include the following table :

Table 1 Features between urban and rural tourism

Urban/Resort Tourism	Rural Tourism
Little open space	Much open space
Settlements over 10,000	Settlements under 10,000
Densely populated	Sparsely populated
Built environment	Natural environment
Many indoor activities	Many outdoor activities
Infrastructure - intensive	Infrastructure - weak
Strong entertainment/retail base	Strong individual activity base
Large establishments	Small establishments
Nationally/Internationally owned firms	Locally owned businesses
Much full time involvement in tourism	Much part-time involvement in tourism
No farm/forestry involvement	Some farm/forestry involvement
Tourism interests self supporting	Tourism supports other interests
Workers may live far from workplace	Workers often live close to workplace
Rarely influenced by seasonal factors	Often influenced by seasonal factors
Many guests	Few guests
Guest relationships anonymous	Guest relationships personal
Professional management	Amateur management
Cosmopolitan in atmosphere	Local in atmosphere
Many modern buildings	Many older buildings
Development/growth ethic	Conservation/limits to growth ethic
General in appeal	Specialist appeal
Broad marketing operation	Niche marketing

Continuum-Concept for Rural Tourism

Commentators seeking to define rurality have made extensive use of the concept of the rural/urban continuum to deal with many different types of area, exhibiting different characteristics, and areas undergoing active change. A similar continuum concept can be useful for those seeking to define rural tourism.

Few areas will display all of the characteristics of rural tourism listed previously. Many will display some "urban" characteristics. Some will be in the process of change and development towards becoming large, urban resorts. The use of the continuum concept allows planners to recognise this trend, and to take steps either to regulate it, or to make infrastructural provision for it.

It can be strongly argued that management strategies in rural tourism should aim to conserve rurality as an important resource. But, in some cases it may be valuable to allow or even encourage some change to take place. Rural tourism cannot be defined solely by holiday type: intensity of use, location, style of management, integration with the community and other factors play an important part in the definition. But a broad-brush approach can be useful.

Again, the continuum concept is a useful one. Many types of holiday can be developed in both urban and rural locations. Holiday-makers may be involved in both urban and rural activities on the same day. A tentative classification of holiday types is given below: it should be used with care. The listing follows the continuum concept, moving from specifically rural to specifically urban with a broad intermediate category.

Traditionally agriculture and forestry were central to rural life. They were the major employers of labour, the main sources of income within the rural economy, and indirectly had a powerful influence on traditions, power structures and life styles. Together, the decisions of farmers and foresters determined rural land use and landscapes.

In the late twentieth century, the central role of farming and forestry has been diminished. Both activities have shed much of their labour force. Only five OECD countries now employ more than 15 per cent of their labour force in farming, forestry and fishing: in eight OECD countries, that figure is less than 5 per cent. The economic power of farming and forestry has declined, not least because those activities are extremely dependent on state subsidies for their profitability.

Traditions are waning before the combined attack of television, power farming techniques and tree processors. Even the role of agri-and arboriculturalists as "landscape gardeners" has diminished: power has begun to move to planners and conservationists.

In this evolving situation, two myths have grown up about the role of rural tourism. One is that rural tourism is farm-based tourism. The second is that diversification into tourism will universally "save" the farming community. These statements are untrue because the relationships between agriculture, forestry and tourism are extremely complex ones.

Farm-based rural tourism has been successful through many (but not all) parts of German-speaking Europe because of a powerful combination of small farm size, interesting scenery, closeness to markets, traditional town/country links caused by late migration from the countryside to city regions, the owner-occupation of farmsteads and the tradition of effective and interventionary local government and co-operative movements.

Furthermore, the role of farm-based tourism has been exaggerated because it has received great attention from both agriculture ministries and academics. The Bibiliography of Rural Tourism for the OECD reveals that farm tourism is the largest single special category of rural tourism in terms of published works. In areas where some or all of the factors mentioned above are lacking, farm-based tourism has been slow to develop. Reasons include:

— Long distances to the urban holiday market;

— Medium and large sized farms which did not need to diversify, or were amalgated to create larger units;

— Rented farms which either failed to receive the owner's permission to diversify, or were amalgamated to create larger units;

— Very poor and very small farms which had no surplus accommodation;

— Coops and local councils and tourist boards which did not help with marketing and infrastructure provision;

— Scenery/heritage/activity attractions which were poor;

— A short, single season.

Thus, for example, over large parts of Eastern England, Sweden, Canada and the United States, farm tourism is poorly developed. But that does not mean that rural tourism is poorly developed. Many of the kinds of rural holidays are not dependent on farm situations. Accommodation can be provided by hotels and motels, small town and village bed and breakfasts, purpose built lodges, camping and caravan sites.

Diversification into rural tourism is frequently held up as a potential panacea for agriculture's ills. There is no doubt that in some areas, and for some businesses, tourism can be valuable. But there are serious problems in its universal application:

Over 75 per cent of the land of the OECD countries is rural: there are insufficient visitors to maintain all farmers in all areas. Farm-based tourism does not reduce productivity on many farms. In some cases, additional tourism earnings are invested to increase agricultural productivity.

Therefore, farm surpluses in OECD countries could continue to grow, leading to falling prices and quota restrictions, and a further round of farm problems. Some areas are unsuitable for intensive tourism development because of remoteness, lack of scenic or heritage attractions, and other factors.

Successful farm tourism development seems to require effective co-operative marketing and development efforts. Many areas have no tradition of co-operation between farmers, or between farmers and governmental agencies. The key relationship in rural tourism is between tourism development and comprehensive rural development, embracing rural services, new enterprise attraction, conservation, a wider role for women and inward investment.

Agriculture has an important role to play in rural tourism, but it is but one facet amongst many: it may be of greater or lesser importance depending on local, regional and national circumstances.

Growth of Rural Tourism

Rural tourism is not an accidental or temporary growth phenomenon. Although the travel trade is in some senses a "fashion" industry, subject to short term trends, the forces behind the growth of rural tourism are more long term in nature. These forces are partly connected to long term changes in the travel market, partly to improvements in transport and communications and partly to the efforts of public agencies charged with assisting rural change.

In total, 14 key factors can be isolated which have been responsible for rural tourism growth in the past and which will continue that growth into the future. Increasing levels of education. The post-war period has seen universal increase in free or assisted education available to the populations of the developed world. This has included longer periods of school-based education, more higher education, the spread of adult and continuing education and the growth of non-formalised education, via radio, television and other media.

Over the last 20 years there has been a boom in the level of interest in heritage both man-made and natural. This reflects many factors: a fear of the future, a fear of rootlessness, better education, time to explore, and, not least, better heritage presentation. Freeman Tilden's pioneering book "Interpreting Our Heritage", first published in 1957 in the United States helped revolutionise and inspire the heritage industry.

Rural areas are especially well suited to heritage interpretation, possessing many historic landscapes, artefacts, and linkages, and fine settings for heritage sites. With the exception of the urban zoo (an institution now in decline), rural areas have a monopoly of the natural heritage market. Increases in leisure time, coupled with higher levels of disposable income, are important factors in developing tourism generally.

The European Community's 1985 Survey of Europeans on Holiday indicated that, of those taking holidays, over one-third now take two or more holiday trips involving overnight stays away from home each year. This is important because while a "traditional" resort-based holiday may still account for main holidays, rural special interest holidays can be tried for the second, often shorter, holiday without too much risk.

Transport and communications have improved so rapidly and universally in the post-war period that remoteness-in time and cost-is now no longer a major problem for rural areas. As a result, rural tourism development projects can now be carried out in places as remote as Canada's Labrador Straits (accessible only from the offshore island of Newfoundland), or the Falkland Islands in the South Atlantic.

This ease of movement owes itself in part to technological changes-jet aircraft, high speed trains, motorways, and roll-on roll-off ferries, automatic telephone systems and fax machines. It has been influenced by better and more widespread money handling facilities, chief of which has been the internationally acceptable credit card. There have also been key attitudinal changes on behalf of both the travel trade and their clients.

Distance and remoteness have become selling points, rather than barriers. Health consciousness has grown and is growing steadily and in the concept of healthy living, active recreation plays an important part. Exercise and sport play central roles in healthy living strategies. Rural areas are well placed to provide outdoor recreation of all kinds from walking to cycling, orienteering, skiing and climbing.

The countryside is assumed to be healthy, with overtones of fresh air and bucolic well-being. In contrast, resort holidays based on the sun/sea/sand formula have been found to offer serious health risks. Medical researchers in Australasia, America and Scandinavia have pinpointed sunbathing as being responsible for higher levels of skin disease, ranging from premature wrinkling to deadly skin cancers.

While this problem is still only fully appreciated in the southern hemisphere, it seems very likely that knowledge of the risks posed by sun-belt holidays will grow. Better outdoor clothing has helped rural holidays in both a practical and a fashion sense. High performance fabrics enable wearers to stay warm and dry in adverse weather, allowing tourists to enjoy wet weather and out-of-season conditions.

Contemporary outdoor clothing is now extremely fashionable, and available in a wide range of colours and styles. Outdoor recreation equipment has also been much improved and many items, such as the mountain bike, the wind surfer and the 4-wheel drive utility vehicle, have achieved cult fashion status.

A growing interest in speciality food is widely evident, be it wild rice from North America, non-pasturized cheeses from France, cholesterol-free, non-farmed salmon and deer from Scandinavia, or organic produce from the Alps. Considerable space in the press is devoted to speciality foods and food preparation. Rural holidays have been able to capitalise on this trend because the countryside is the source of quality non-processed foods.

Green issues have risen high on most political agendas over the last ten years. This interest has been seized upon by the marketeers of many consumer products, including holiday tour operators. Rural holidays, although not necessarily environmentally friendly, can capitalise on the wholesomeness which the countryside is felt to exude.

Authenticity is a quality which is increasingly prized. In a world of video and television entertainment, factory produced goods, and suburban anonymity, the authenticity of the countryside, and the personal touch provided by small scale communities and accommodation units is extremely valuable.

A 1986 survey of the German holiday market found that "to switch off, relax" was the number one aim of those taking holidays: this aim was given by 66 per cent of respondents. 47 per cent wished to experience nature, and 32 per cent sought cleaner air and an unpolluted environment. Ageing but active populations are becoming the norm across the OECD countries. Early retirement is now commonplace, as are active 70-year-olds.

In 1971 83 per cent of British males aged 60-64 were still working in full time jobs. By 1995 it is expected that only 55 per cent of men in that age group will remain in full time work. Effective occupational pensions allow this active but ageing population to travel widely: many choose rural holidays for health reasons and to discover new non-urban experiences.

The many facets of rural tourism are specially placed to fulfil the needs of this growth market. Individualism is also a growth market, rejecting the mass activities of the past. The growth of individualism has been noted and acted upon by the car manufacturers, by clothing manufacturers, and by many other purveyors of consumer goods.

Rural tourism, because of the fragmented and small scale nature of the enterprises involved, is especially capable of exploiting this market trend, although high quality selling and hospitality skills are needed. The rural agencies, numerous in most countries, have been quick to express an interest in rural tourism and to offer aid and advice. These agencies include those connected with agriculture, with nature conservation, with community welfare, with the arts and crafts, with National Parks, with economic development, transport-the list is almost endless.

Although the agencies rarely co-ordinate their activities, and are rarely organisations with any experience of tourism, they have assisted many collective projects and individual enterprises. There is very little quantitative knowledge of the precise size of the rural tourism market. Estimates have been made of the size of the "Special Interest" tourism market, which is a closely related area.

The World Tourism Organization estimated the special interest market to be about 3 per cent of the total domestic and international market in 1985. In 1989, a survey of U.S. travel agents revealed that special interest holidays comprised 15 per cent of all bookings. Other U.S. surveys show that eco-tourists (a related niche rural tourism market) are relatively wealthy, and spend more per holiday than conventional visitors. Therefore, if levels of income and educational attainment continue to rise across the OECD countries, the market for rural tourism should also grow.

Aside from the bird-watching and hunting/fishing markets, which have a wider appeal across the whole socio-economic spectrum in many countries, rural tourism is generally supported by an up-market clientele.

The American state of Wyoming (with a population of 512 000) estimates that wildlife tourism is worth over $ 1 billion annually within its borders. Clearly, rural tourism, while still only a minority tourism market, is already making a valuable contribution to rural economies. Its contribution can be expressed not only in financial terms, but also in terms of jobs, contributions towards funding conservation, encouragement to the adoption of new working practices, and the injection o a new vitality into sometimes weakened economies. Job retention is extremely important in rural areas where mployment decline is often endemic. Tourism cash

ows can assist job retention in services such as reta ling, transport, hospitality and medical care. It can also provide additional income for farmers, and, in some cases, for foresters and fisherman. Job retention is not as politically glamorous as job creation, ut, by helping the viability of small communities, it is critical to the survival of marginal areas. Studie of rural Austria, Sweden and Ireland have documented t e role of tourism in job retentio

Job creation is a further possibility if rural tour sm is successful. Job creation typically occurs in the hot l and catering trades, but can also take place in transport retailing, and in information/heritage interpretation. Studies in Britain suggest that job creation varies by enterprise type.

Farmhouse accommodation and bed-and-breakfast can create up to 23 jobs per £ 100 000 of tourism revenue. Job creation effects are less marked in hotels and caravan/campsites, yielding approximately six jobs per £ 100 000 of revenue. Job diversity is encouraged by rural tourism development.

Most rural areas have little job variety outside farming and basic services. Better job diversity enriches rural society, and helps retain population levels. Pluriactivity can be a further useful by-product of tourism in the countryside. Pluriactivity is the term used when an individual or family carries out more than one type of job to maintain their income. A part-time farmer could also offer accommodation, assist the local administration in service tasks and act as a ski-instructor.

Sea fishermen may take tourist parties on angling trips, on whale watching expeditions off the coast of Canada and the United States, or on bird-watching excursions off the coast of Ireland or Scotland. Pluriactivity guards against recession in any one sector. It is especially important in the rural context because of the cultural importance of the family as a unit in many traditional societies.

Service retention is vital in rural areas: rural tourism can assist in three ways. Visitor information services can be provided by existing outlets, such as shops, thus increasing income flows if payment is made for acting as information outlets. Services can also benefit by the additional customers which visitors provide. The high levels of public transport in rural Austria and Switzerland are in part due to the support they receive from holiday-makers.

This additional custom is not, however, automatic: to make the most of the potential, services often need to offer new products, to be available at different times and to understand the new markets. Finally, tourism's importance to national economies can strengthen the political case for subsides to help retain services. Farm support is a major issue on all political agendas.

Many studies have shown that farm incomes can be bolstered by rural tourism, through accommodation enterprises of all kinds, by developing open farms and other attractions, by increased sales of farm produce, and by increasing female activity rates through additional off-farm employment. There are widespread variations in the levels of farmer participation in rural tourism throughout the OECD countries, varying by region, farm size, age of farmer and other factors.

Economic benefits are of first importance in prompting farmers to enter tourism enterprises, the surveys also stress that many farmers achieve a social bonus. Visitors bring variety and company to what can be a lonely and limited life style. Forestry is an important activity in many upland and climatically marginal regions. Forest regions have suffered serious socio-economic problems in recent years, partly because of the mechanisation of tree felling and processing, and partly because of falling prices following reduced timber demand.

Rural tourism can assist forestry by diversifying income sources for forest communities if the special qualities of the forest environment for recreational use are realised and developed. Landscape conservation has become an increasingly important form of heritage protection. Although this dates back to the designation of America's Yellowstone National Park in 1872, the national park movement is still progressing and most countries now have a wide range of lesser designations covering many types of landscape.

Landscape is of crucial importance to rural tourism but, equally, visitor use is vital to the landscape conservation industry. Visitor use brings political benefits, can bring economic gains, and can provide jobs in maintaining and repairing traditional landscapes worn by recreational activities. Smaller settlements in the countryside have always been at greater risk of losing viability because they are unable to support the many services which now require larger threshold populations to support them.

Rural tourism can assist these smaller settlements to survive, because smaller places have a special attraction for visitors. Careful management of this process is, however, required. Rural arts and crafts have a special place in the cultural heritage of regions and nations. Many commentators have noted that tourism can assist arts and crafts, both by recognising their importance, and by purchasing craft products. Income flows from these activities are well documented. Support between the arts and tourism can be a two-way process.

Many communities now use arts and crafts festivals as a marketing mechanism to encourage visitors to come to their areas. Cultural provision has always been restricted in rural areas. The lack of major facilities such as theatre, opera, music and galleries has been one of the many factors encouraging rural depopulation. Nature conservation, like landscape conservation, is a stated goal of most modern governments. It is, however, an expensive process.

Rural tourism can valorise nature conservation in a monetary sense. Many estimates have been made of the value of nature to tourism. On the grand scale, it is estimated that each elephant is worth $ 14 375 to the Kenyan economy. On a lesser scale, the British Royal Society for the Protection of Birds has demonstrated that even small bird reserves can help sustain village shops by visitor purchases and by the expenditure of reserve management and maintenance staff. Visitors are prepared to pay to see nature: most reserves and many national parks successfully charge for entrance. How far charging can be extended is a much discussed point in conservation circles.

The historic built environment can benefit from rural tourism in two ways.

— Many historic properties now charge for admission in order to maintain their fabrics and surrounding gardens and parklands.
— There are important buildings from the past which have become redundant.

Churches have lost their congregations, castles have lost their wars, farm buildings have become too small for modern equipment, railway stations have lost their trains, and canal warehouses no longer have barge traffic. The tourist industry can usually use these redundant bu ldings profitably and imaginatively: they can becom attractions in their own right. Environmental improv ments such as village paving and traffic regulation schemes, sewage and litter disposal can be assisted by tourism revenues and political pressures from tourism authorities. These help develop pride of place, important in retaining existing population and businesses, and in attracting new enterprises and families. Small fishing communities are suffering badly from dwindling fish stocks, quota restrictions and international bans on some activities.

A number of these communities can successfully diversify into sports fishing, bird and seal watching, and coastal sightseeing. Some environmental groups claim that potential revenue from whale and dolphin watching could exceed revenue from catching whales for meat. The role of women within the rural community was, in the past, a restricted one. Farming, forestry and mining were very much male occupations. Alternative jobs for women were few.

Women were rarely involved in local politics. The widespread emancipation of women, coupled with the possibilities which rural tourism offers, have together done much in many areas to release the under-utilised talents and energies of the female half of the population. Studies show that tourism enterprises have increased the power of women within both the family and the community. Experience in Spain, Greece, France, Britain and Ireland has demonstrated how the flexible and open-minded approach of women towards new ideas and co-operative working has helped develop and lead successful rural tourism projects.

The development of the role of women could do much for the economic and social well-being of many rural areas. New ideas and initiatives will be essential if rural communities are to prosper into the twenty-first century. Efforts to support agriculture, forestry and service provision by state subsidies have done much to develop a culture of dependency within the countryside.

The new challenges and the fiercely competitive nature of the tourism market could do much to encourage enterprise and new methods. There is also evidence that rural tourism can act as a catalyst to bring new businesses of many kinds into rural communities. Research in the English county of Cornwall shows that good holiday experiences by business people were instrumental in encouraging them to re-locate their businesses to the county.

Problems in Rural Tourism

Since 1971, the area has been able to reverse a century of depopulation, and it is now experiencing a population renewal. While many benefits can flow from rural tourism development, there can be problems. All economic structural re-alignments can disrupt sensitive environments. And, as the records of numerous rural aid agencies will testify, rural communities can be extremely resistant to new ideas. The problems in developing and managing rural tourism are listed below:

— *The environmental threat*: Rural tourism operates within sensitive natural environments. Some of the most attractive tourism destinations have the most sensitive environments. These include sea and lake shorelines, wetlands, high mountain areas, and polar areas. Many studies have highlighted the threats which tourism has already brought to the environment.

Intensive skiing has destroyed vegetation and encouraged land-slips; climbing erodes rock faces, and, with modern equipment, destroys their natural condition; walking and riding wears out paths in heavily used areas; noise and litter drive out and injure wild creatures; existing farming practices are upset by fire, dogs and competition for labour. The peace, quiet and authentic nature of the countryside can be seriously compromised. All these issues can be tackled to some extent by the skilled management of the countryside; management of the order required is as yet rarely available.

— *The socio-cultural threat*: Just as the influx of large numbers of visitors can disrupt the natural world, so also can visitors impinge upon the small scale, static, and well ordered socio-cultural world of the rural community. Earnings patterns change, success/failure relationships are altered, power structures are challenged. More fundamentally, sociologists have long recognised that the impact of "advanced" cultures on "traditional" cultures almost always brings change to the traditional culture and not in the other direction.

This process has been examined in detail in the Mediterranean and in the Alpine lands. But the process is most marked where special ethnic or linguistic groups are involved. The Irish-speaking Gaeltacht areas of Ireland have long experience of the problem: a recent positive step towards an answer has been the appointment of a project officer to try to develop tourism which is friendly towards the Irish language. In North America, the relationship of the Indian tribes and Inuit peoples to tourism development is a difficult issue still in the process of reassessment.

— *The housing question*: Some successful rural tourism areas-in the Canadian Rockies, in South-West England, in parts of the Alps-have found that success in the visitor market has brought accommodation problems for local people. Small communities rarely have very much surplus housing. If they are to retain their character they must not expand too much or too rapidly. Visitor demand has three types of effect.

  Housing can be taken over for visitor accommodation, usually in the self-catering sector. Housing purchased as second-homes by city people is often rarely used, and brings little economic benefit to the local community. Housing can be purchased as retirement homes by holidaymakers who fall in love with their holiday areas. On retirement, the one-time holidaymakers gradually create a tendency towards a gerontocracy. All these impacts raise prices and create tension within rural societies.

— *The incoming entrepreneur*: Many local farmers and businesses do not decide to enter the tourism market when opportunities present themselves. Surveys show that, in extreme cases, up to 80 per cent of tourism-related busineses in small towns and villages are owned, managed or controlled by incoming or non-local entrepreneurs.

In some respects incomers can provide a valuable transfusion of contacts, capital and skill. But they can also present problems. They may be insensitive to local tradition, cultures, working practices and architectural styles. They may use non-local suppliers for goods and services. They may repatriate their profits and capital gains out of the area. They have little loyalty to their new base of operations and often leave when trading conditions deteriorate. Less tangibly, but equally important, they set up tensions between locals and incomers, and do little to change the dependency culture common to many rural places.

Traffic congestion-usually road traffic, but in some cases sea and air traffic-can be a major problem if an area is successful in attracting tourists. Narrow roads can easily be choked by traffic both inside and outside settlements, parking becomes an issue, non-tourism business can suffer and, in extreme cases, emergency services cannot make urgent calls.

The attractiveness of the area as a destination can decline, taking it down-market. There can be side effects on landscape and nature conservation. Traffic management techniques and better use of public transport can help, but the funds and skills necessary are not usually available. The issues of planning, local control, public participation and partnership bring together many of the points covered so far in this section.

In an ideal world, local people and businesses would control tourism development in such a way that the problems discussed earlier would be minimised and benefits maximised. Planning controls would ensure a carefully worked out balance of development between tourism-related and other land uses. Different types of tourism activity would be zoned into the regions best suited for those types of development.

Employers and employees would undertake regular training courses to learn the skills of marketing, hospitality, interpretation and tourism planning. The community would feel that it had "ownership" of its industry in a broad sense. As a result the visitor would feel a genuine sense of welcome from the host population. But real world is rarely ideal. The financial power of the incoming entrepreneur, and the power of skilled outsiders including tour operators and tourist board officials, means that local control is seldom achieved.

When locals do have power, they often do not have the foresight, experience or skills necessary. In some areas local politicians resent and resist development. In others, the promise of new jobs and income can be too great a temptation, leading to the acceptance of damaging schemes. In most cases tourism management is not practised because of cost and political implications.

There have, however, been many experiments in introducing local participation into rural tourism development projects. Most are so recent that evaluation is not yet complete. Canada has pioneered the most widespread attempts at community participation in rural tourism planning. Alberta has been especially active in this field, initiating its Community Tourism Action Plan, involving 426 out of 429 eligible communities, in 1987.

Local committees have been encouraged and assisted to draw up tourism development plans through extensive consultation. Similar actions have been carried out in British Columbia and Saskatchewan. Heritage Canada has been involved in exemplary local participation work in Labrador. While it is difficult to assess the results of this work at this stage, it is already becoming clear that there are widespread variations in the quality of the plans produced.

Regional co-ordination has been found to be necessary and is now being developed. Much has been learned about how to assist the work of local committees as a result of these experiences. Other important efforts at establishing local control have taken place in Britain, Ireland and Switzerland. In Switzerland, the community of Waltensburg successfully built and operates a 70-bed hotel, to high environmental standards, with profits flowing to assist other local development schemes.

In Britain and Ireland, project leaders have assisted communities and districts to grapple with control and planning issues. In some areas comprehensive community businesses have been formed to ensure local control and profit retention. The Connemara West Company, based in Letterfrack, Galway, Ireland is an oft quoted example. Community business, however, seems to be successful only in special circumstances.

Over 75 per cent of the land area of the OECD is rural. It seems unlikely that all of this vast area can participate in tourism development. Some types of area have important natural advantages for rural tourism. Experience suggests that six factors are involved in determining the suitability of areas for investment purposes.

But some studies also suggests that these factors are not exclusive, and that because the tourist industry is highly dynamic, and subject to changes in fashion, the factors may not remain constant in the future. Furthermore, an area's possession of any one-or even all- of these factors does not guarantee success. The factors are:

— Scenic value-including mountains, seashores, lakes, islands, rivers and special interest scenery such as wetlands or mixed deciduous forest.

— Special wildlife assets.

— Cultural assets including historic buildings/towns/villages/sites and/or ethnic heritage of all types.

— Special facilities for sports including hunting, fishing, skiing, hiking etc.

— Ease of access by large populations.

— Effective promotional, commercial and management skills.

The OECD Rural Development Programme's typology for rural areas differentiates between remote areas, intermediate areas and economically integrated areas. The typology forms a useful additional set of criteria to consider when assessing conditions for the growth of tourism activities.

The economically integrated areas are usually close to large cities, offering considerable leisure market potential. Closeness to cities may, however, result in a higher level of day-visit recreational use, which is less valuable in financial terms than overnight stays. Remote areas are, by definition, more likely to attract guests who stay overnight, leading to greater net revenue potential per visitor. If teamed with mountain or lake scenery, remoteness-if not too daunting-can be a considerable attraction. But remoteness without fine scenery generally means that there will be little likelihood of rural tourism development.

The OECD Rural Development Programme typology can also be a valuable indicator when considering the likelihood of local people taking up new initiatives such as tourism. Peripheral areas may try new enterprises because of a high "desperation factor", brought about by poverty and decline. Economically integrated areas may, paradoxically, also be keen to try new enterprises-not because of desperation, but because of spare capital and the large potential markets nearby. It is in the intermediate areas that it can be most difficult to change attitudes and develop new tourism businesses.

Farmers are critical in maintaining both the basic rural economy and the scenery on which rural tourism depends. Yet farmers have responded unevenly and often only slowly to the opportunities available through tourism. Some farmers are strongly anti-tourist, resenting visitors on their territory, especially where footpaths or riding trails cross their land. Many would prefer better prices for farm produce rather than incentives to move into the visitor industry.

When farmers do diversify into tourism, they often do so together with other farmers, rather than with local communities, and thus potential co-operative benefits are lost. At the root of many of the problems encountered in involving farmers in tourism is a basic question of knowledge and training. A hotelier would be incapable of working in the farming industry without a lengthy period of training, yet farmers (or their wives) are expected to diversify into providing visitor services of all kinds with little or no training.

Training deficiencies are not confined to agriculturalists. Many business people and employees working in rural tourism have little or no training in the many skills required for this complex and competitive industry. Lack of training is one of the reasons why some studies have noted a high incidence of business failures in the rural tourism field.

Failure to group and to set up co-operative ventures is a common but not universal problem. Because rural tourism enterprises are small, co-operation with other businesses can bring major savings in marketing and training and in the purchase of supplies. Co-operative groupings can also negotiate with government bodies to fund infrastructural improvements, and can work with the major players in the international tourism market, the tour operators.

Interest and success in co-operative ventures owes much to the history and experience of the regions concerned. Where there is a tradition of co-operation, usually in farming, tourism co-operatives seem to work.

Managing Rural Tourism

The expansion of modern tourism has not been the product of planning but of a largely free market. Tourism is a consumer industry: central planning in this area has had an uneven record. There is the claim that the tourism industry is different-it is unmanageable. In the words of Professor Butler of the University of Western Ontario, Canada-"tourism development is like pregnancy-one cannot become just a little bit pregnant". The case for managing rural tourism rests on four points.

First, the tourist industry is now well established and mature. Clients are more discerning and many seek a carefully managed, quality environment on holiday, rather than just a holiday. The industry is beginning to realise that it has long term environmental responsibilities, and management techniques can help it to meet those responsibilities.

Second, rural tourism is different from resort tourism because it operates in a very sensitive human and fragile physical environment. Management is, therefore, essential if the very qualities on which the rural holiday relies are not to be lost through inappropriate or overdevelopment.

Third, because of the many new and inexperienced small enterprises involved in the rural tourism sector, some unifying strategy is essential for business planning purposes. The initial development of this new sector frequently requires public sector finance; some form of strategic plan is normally necessary to gain access to that finance.

Finally, tourism management is beginning to evolve into something more flexible and enterprise-orientated than simple land use and infrastructure planning. This process may still have a long way to go, but most commentators and many experienced members of the industry see management as a necessary future tool. On balance, therefore, it seems that there is a powerful case for the creation of rural tourism management strategies.

Rural tourism development and management has three distinct sources. Recreation management ideas have evolved in North America over the last 50 years, largely through national park administrations. Key areas of discussion centre around visitor and vehicle control, zoning policies, wildlife and vegetation management, trail design and maintenance, carrying capacity assessment and interpretation policies.

Most of these ideas are useful to rural tourism management but the recreational management approach is essentially non-commercial and does not, therefore, answer many of the question which rural tourism management poses. Recreational management techniques were usually evolved in non-farmed areas, free of settlements of any size, and in areas where land ownership was in the hands of the managing authorities. The authorities usually had considerable powers of planning control, and long term funding to carry out their ideas.

The concept of sustainable tourism was developed in the alpine regions of Europe by German, Swiss, Austrian, French and Italian academics, conservationists and tourism professionals. It is known by a number of other names green tourism, responsible tourism, post-industrial tourism, meta-tourism and alternative tourism are but a few. It was developed as an answer to the pressing problems of mass tourism in the Alps and the Mediterranean. It can best be described as a system of long term tourism planning which is friendly towards the long term well-being of communities and habitats, the visitor, and the tourist industry. It envisages these three players in the tourism equation being in a triangular relationship.

In unplanned mass tourism, the industry dominates decision making, to the detriment of all parties because of the operation of the "resort cycle" theory, which envisages that a resort will have a finite life because of eventual overcrowding and deterioration. The Sustainability Concept gives power and knowledge in equal amounts to each party, resulting in careful, slow optimisation of each other's aims.

Sustainable tourism is a powerfully attractive concept to the rural tourism manager. It provides a useful philosophy and checklist for proposed actions. Because of its all-embracing scope, because of its utopian aims, and because it is still new, it remains largely untested over time. A number of British, Austrian and other areas are now implementing sustainable rural tourism strategies.

Rural tourism project management is also in its infancy, but over the last ten years there have been many rural tourism development projects throughout the world. These have been variable in aims and quality. They have been handled by a variety of professionals including community social workers, economic development officers, marketeers, educationalists, historians and interpretation experts, land use planners, and farm advisors.

Most projects have been of short duration-up to three years-and many have been unable to develop tangible long lasting benefits in that time. Rural tourism management in the future should try to combine the experience and knowledge of all the sources discussed above. But much more work is required before long term effectiveness and success can be achieved.

Over the last 20 years, many businesses and communities have participated in the growth of tourism in rural areas. But several important problems remain to be addressed before the development of rural tourism is fully understood and before the benefits of that development are available to all regions in all countries.

Perhaps the most important issue is how a sustainable form of rural tourism can be developed-a form of tourism which would retain the intrinsic values of the countryside, while sustaining its economic life, and helping ensure the long-term profitability of the travel industry interests involved in the transfer of visitors both inter-regionally and internationally.

Rural tourism strategists need to determine their aims before commencing development; those aims should be reviewed periodically. To recognise that there will be a need for special partnership arrangements to help rural areas develop tourism. These partnerships may be between businesses, between businesses and the community, and between businesses, communities and public sector institutions. They will be necessary because of the fragility of the rural world itself, and the fragility of many of its small enterprises.

They will be necessary because of the need to restructure the rural economy. And the partnership concept will also be necessary because of the peculiar nature of tourism itself in a rural area. Tourism is a special form of economic activity in any area because of its powerful impact on the public domain. While car manufacturing or office work can be hidden away in industrial estates or science parks, tourism's basic acts of sightseeing, shopping and touring are totally public.

In rural areas there is an additional intrusion: tourism frequently intrudes onto the private domain, as visitors seek access to private land, to private lakesides and sea shore. Partnerships between interests are, therefore, vital to deal with the conflicts of interest which can easily arise.

Successful development and management will require both public and private sector participation. Traditionally, public sector involvement in rural areas has been very considerable, both because of the need to conserve and control national food supplies and because of the long term structural weaknesses within the rural economy. Because of this inherited position, and because there seems little likelihood of most rural economies strengthening in the near future, the public sector's role will continue to be a powerful one.

But tourism in non-rural areas is essentially a private sector initiative, and experience shows that it functions best in private hands. Therefore, while there will always be a strong regulatory and co-ordinating role for the public sector within rural tourism, steps should be taken wherever possible to stimulate private sector involvement. Public sector involvement is likely to be greatest in the early stages of an area's development, with private sector responsibilities then gradually taking on a more important role.

Lack of market knowledge, and lack of knowledge about how to relate to markets, are common problems for many rural tourism initiatives. The two parts to this issue are:

— The need to understand the size, location, characteristics, perception and requirements of markets;

— The need to understand how to relate to, influence and win markets via marketing campaigns, liaison with travel agents, travel companies and tour operators.

It is most likely that basic market research is best initiated and funded by the public sector in order to ensure that this fundamental information is available to all businesses. Marketing campaigns and promotions may be begun by the public sector, but the role of that sector should gradually change to one of co-ordinator rather than funder as development proceeds.

The development of regional and local sustainable rural tourism strategy plans to assess an area's strengths, weaknesses, opportunities and threats, to guide both public and private sector investment, and to assess environmental and community requirements. This is usually a public sector responsibility, but requires close consultation with the private sector and with environmental and community interests.

The development of an ongoing monitoring and evaluation process to review the success of tourism as an industry, and to provide a response mechanism for environmental and community interests. This is usually a private/public sector partnership, with a secretariat provided by the public sector.

Lack of accommodation or of suitable accommodation is one of the key development problems in many rural tourism areas. Accommodation is essentially a private sector responsibility, but it may require advice / grant aid in the early stages. Quality control may be a public sector responsibility, but some of the quality control systems can be devolved to industry associations as development proceeds.

Although the rural world is itself the key attraction, there are many cases where special emphasis can be given to aspects of rurality by the careful development of visitor attractions. These developments are normally private sector responsibilities. The role of the public sector is that of guidance, encouragement/ discouragement, regulation and, in special cases, grant aid may be necessary: in peripheral areas community-based developments may be both necessary and useful.

Transportation facilities and services-either a public or private sector responsibility, although rural public transport is often assisted by public subsidy even if provided by private operators. Information facilities-usually, but not always or necessarily, a public sector provision. In some rural areas the private sector can be very effective at providing information on a franchised basis from a public authority.

Interpretation of landscape, heritage, nature. These facilities are typically a public sector responsibility, especially if carried out for a wider region. Private provision is also possible, either as a form of private visitor attraction, or as part of the work of special interest groups. Environmental protection and repair is normally a public sector responsibility. Payment for protection, and especially for repair, is however, a difficult issue: the principle of "the polluter pays" is increasingly threatened or invoked by the public sector in an effort to reduce the charge on the public purse. These problems, if unresolved, can produce serious disagreements between the community, the tourist trade and visitors.

Research and development is important in all industries: it is particularly important in a new field like rural tourism. Research can find ways of lessening the impact of tourism on the environment and new ways of attracting and retaining visitors, and can help keep areas in the front rank of the internationally competitive business of tourism. Normally, research will be led by the public sector, but private sector participation is extremely important if the work is to be relevant and acted upon.

Many small businesses and numerous public sector organisations are involved in rural tourism. The successful promotion of development and management planning requires more than usually informed, skilled and dedicated leadership. This is an intangible factor, but one of great importance. It can help persuade business interests to be kinder to the environment; it can steer difficult government institutions to more pragmatic interpretations of their roles; it can influence the doubting farmer; it can bring new ideas to communities of no hope.

Leadership can be provided by enlightened individuals from the private sector, by politicians, by public sector agencies, by local/regional administrations and administrators, by tourist boards, and by powerful land owners; what is important is that there be leadership, that it be carefully fostered not feared, and that it be fostered in depth, so that when one individual or agency fails, the whole momentum of development is not lost. A number of North American educational institutions provide short courses in leadership for rural politicians and administrators.

Rural tourism is still a relatively new area of business, and, therefore, much basic research is needed. That basic research is especially critical because of the highly competitive nature of the free enterprise tourism market. The countryside may have intrinsic advantages because of the growth of special interest, independent holiday-making, but existing resorts and mass tourism enterprises are already researching how best to improve their marketing and their products to regain market share.

In almost all business sectors research and development involves a partnership between the public and private sectors. The need for partnership is very important if rural tourism and its development are to succeed. Rural areas and enterprises have a history of public sector intervention. Rural tourism is growing in a fragmented and ad hoc way: public sector partnerships can co-ordinate activities.

Since many of rural tourism's activities take place in the public domain, careful research into environmental and visitor management is necessary to maintain established community goals such as landscape, nature and heritage protection during the re-structuring of the rural economy away from primary production towards a greater reliance on the service sector.

Market information studies for rural tourism are few, and this is a major problem in determining the size, characteristics and requirements of the market. Without this information, it is difficult to plan infrastructure investment, to provide effective business training, to encourage suitable numbers and types of new entrants into rural tourism provision and, of course, to develop marketing campaigns.

Market information studies need to cover market groups already taking rural holidays, and those who do not. For both groups, basic positioning information should include age/family size/occupational characteristics/area of origin/holiday patterns during current year and previous years/ perceived requirements of holidays/likely accommodation type/likely method of travel/method of choosing holidays/knowledge and perçeption of specified "control" areas.

For those not taking rural holidays, additional questions should cover reasons why alternatives were taken, perception of specific types of rural holiday, perception of specific rural areas, and likely future trends in holiday choice. For those taking rural holidays, additional questions should review propensity to take holidays in various types of rural area, repeat visit likelihood, major strengths and weaknesses of previous rural holidays, the importance of various types of infrastructure, and likely future trends in holiday choice.

The development of a standard way of obtaining and analysing this market information would assist rural groups with limited skills and resources, and also enable inter-regional and international comparisons to be made. Rural tourism areas often-but not always-have weak and amateur links to their markets. There would be value in the publication of an evaluated good-practice guide looking at a range of successful areas and the techniques they have employed to relate to their markets.

Rural tourism investment is undertaken largely to improve the economic, environmental and social well being of rural areas. Relatively little is known about the levels of return on different types of investment: almost nothing is known about the long term impact of less tangible forms of investment such as training, strategy planning etc. Typical problems faced by investment planners in rural areas are gaps in knowledge on returns from:

— Display boards;

— tourism information centres;

— visitor and heritage centres;

— craft workshops and galleries;

— on-road cycle route provision;

— off-road cycle route provision;

— public transport enhancement;

— scenic road construction;

— training in business skills;

— training in hospitality skills;

— strategy planning exercises.

The OECD's Rural Development Programme has an ongoing project to devise internationally acceptable indicators to measure the work of rural development programmes. Any research on the benefits flowing from rural tourism development should, where possible, be linked with the project on rural indicators to ensure international compatibility and comparability.

The quality of the natural and human environment is an important asset for tourism to the countryside. Much is written about the need to sustain the qualities involved: most of that writing is in generalised terms. In 1992 the World Tourism Organization (WTO) set up an International Working Group on Indicators of Sustainable Tourism.

The working group reported to the WTO's Environment Committee in early 1993. It recommended the development of a series of measures and indicators of sustainability, including warning indicators, pressure/stress indicators, measures of management impact, and destination attractivity indices. Indicators were felt to be necessary at national level, and also for critical areas/"hot spots". It also recommended pilot testing of these indicators at a number of sites during 1993/4.

Collaborative research with the WTO on sustainability indicators for rural tourism would be extremely valuable. It would help back up the economic assessments already mentioned as research areas. It would give firm guidelines for decisions on management and control policies. It would help provide protection against overdevelopment and loss of a unique selling point: rurality.

Training is accepted as important in all spheres of economic activity. Training in rural tourism is generally poorly developed: this is a major stumbling block to development. Rural tourism requires relatively little new capital: the physical landscape, natural and built heritage, farming pattern, and, in many cases, redundant buildings, are all there.

But, successful rural tourism requires totally new skills: in marketing, in hospitality, in catering, in heritage interpretation and guidance, in visitor management, in festival and event promotion, in building conversion, and in rural tourism strategy planning itself. A number of organisations have begun to develop training programmes. These include:

— The United Nations Food and Agricultural Organisation through its Rome Office;

— COFRAT (Comité de formation des ruraux aux activities du tourisme) in France's Loire-Atlantique Region;

— In Austria, the OEAR, the Österreichische Arbeitsgemeinschaft für Eigenständige Regionalentwicklung (the Austrian Association for Regional Development through Self-Help);

— The University of Bristol's Rural Tourism Unit in the United Kingdom;

— The University of Minnesota's Tourism Center in the United States: this organisation has developed manuals and videos, and hosted a national interactive tele-conference. It was the base for America's National Rural Tourism Development Project from 1988 to 1991;

— The University of Calgary in Canada, in its Management Faculty, through Continuing Education, and through the specialist Center for Livable Communities.

Training has tended to concentrate on small businesses and employees. It has usually been short term, with little linkage between courses, and no long term training plan. Existing business courses have usually been adapted: little specifically tailor-made material has been produced on rural tourism.

Training for rural tourism professionals, planners and administrators is less well developed. The market is smaller, but paradoxically, the need is probably greater. Planners and professionals are the industry's leaders, acting as brokers between businesses, between businesses and politicians, and frequently, between businesses and markets.

One of the keys to this development would be the setting up of an international Rural Tourism Training Network, bringing institutions and agencies together to learn of each others' skills, successes and failures, and common problems. The network would avoid duplication of research effort, and bring the hybrid vigour which can often stem from such collaborative ventures. The network need not be fully global, but could also function concurrently on a continental scale with groups in Europe, North America, Australasia and Asia.

Community involvement and community/industry co-operation are special features of rural tourism in some places. They can bring local capital investment into play, can lessen conflicts between visitor interests and local interests, and can contribute towards the authenticity of rural holidays which many visitors seek. Yet community involvement is unsuccessful in some places, while very valuable in others.

Many public sector agencies are involved in rural tourism development, management and marketing. Few of the agencies involved were designed specifically to work on rural tourism, or, in many cases, on tourism of any kind. Examples of their diverse origins include agricultural advisory services, national park authorities, regional and local planning agencies, state forestry authorities, rural development agencies, local government planning services, leisure services and general administrative services, and, of course, all embracing tourist boards ranging from national through regional to local level.

Some public sector involvement in tourism and development in rural areas will probably always be needed. Whether, however, public sector agencies should carry out the full range of roles, or should be limited to a regulatory function, is not clear. Certainly, in some areas, co-operatives, semi-state agencies and private consultancies carry out roles reserved elsewhere for the state sector.

International co-operation can yield valuable insights into problems and act as a powerful educational device. Many international agencies are already involved in rural tourism, including OECD, FAO, the Council of Europe, ECOVAST, EUROTER, the European Community, some travel trade groups and informal organisations such as the Anglo-American Countryside Stewardship consortium. This area of research would look at what international links already exist and how they operate. It would examine the success (or otherwise) of different types of co-operation and exchange, and consider ways of co-ordinating schemes, and expanding (or contracting) them where advantageous.

According to estimates from the World Development Report 2000/2001, almost half of the world's 6 billion inhabitants live on less than US$2 a day, and a fifth live below the international poverty line - less than US$1 a day. While the number of people who live below the poverty line declined between 1987 and 1998 in some regions - most notably East Asia and the Pacific - in most developing countries the number continues to rise.

Poverty is particularly acute in South Asia and sub-Saharan Africa, which are home respectively to 43.5% and 24.3% of the people in the developing world who subsist on less than US$1 a day. While extreme income poverty persists in many developing countries, they have also experienced considerable growth in international tourist arrivals and receipts.

During 1998/1999, East Asia experienced a growth rate in tourism arrivals of 11.1%, the Middle East 16.2%, Africa 7.8%, and South Asia 8.3%, all of which are well above the global average of 4.0%. Between 1990 and 1997, tourism was either an important sector of the economy, or growing rapidly in almost half of the low income countries, and in virtually all of the lower-middle income countries.

Tourism is significant in eleven of the twelve countries which hold 80% of the world's poor. Moreover, tourism has become the world's leading source of export earnings, if international tourism receipts and international fare receipts are combined. In light of these statistics, some analysts believe that the tourism industry can play a significant role in poverty reduction.

Many studies report on the general impacts of tourism in developing countries, whether social, cultural, economic, or environmental. However there is no research on specific initiatives being implemented by different actors (governments, donors, NGOs, private companies, and community groups) to make tourism more 'pro-poor', nor on the impacts that these have had on various 'poor groups.'

Poverty is a multidimensional phenomenon that consists of a 'lack' of certain things upon which human health, well-being, and autonomous social functioning depend, including the ability to meet 'basic needs' (i.e., food, shelter, clothing, etc.). This lack may consist of insufficient income, consumption or assets, entitlements, rights, or security. Thus, there are both material and non-material dimensions to poverty.

A consensus among donors has established an international poverty line which distinguishes the 'poor' as those who live on less than US$2 per day (in 1985 terms adjusted for purchasing power parity), while people living on less than US$1 per day are classified as 'extremely poor.' International development targets call for the reduction by half of the proportion of people who live in extreme poverty by 2015.

While the international poverty line is useful for stimulating political action and for measuring progress according to a specific dimensions of poverty, it is based on a reductionist conceptualisation of poverty. Consumption-based indicators tend to be more reliable for measuring the material dimensions of poverty because they can assess shifts in the quantity of things that people use, which do not necessarily correlate with monetary income.

Assets-based approaches include material and non-material dimensions that are discussed as forms of capital. Poverty can consist of insufficient material assets like physical and environmental capital (e.g., facilities, land and natural resources) as well as financial capital (e.g., money and credit), or a lack of non-material assets like human capital (e.g., education, skills) and social capital (e.g., organisational networks and organisational strength).

Insufficient access to or ability to develop various types of capital at times is related to one or more entitlement failures. The concept of entitlements gained recognition through the work of Amartya Sen on famines, but it is relevant to poverty reduction theory in general. Essentially, an entitlement is a claim upon resources that is sanctioned by formal or informal socio-cultural, political, legal, or economic mechanisms.

An 'entitlement failure' occurs when those mechanisms deny certain people access to the resources upon which they depend for their health and well-being. Thus, for Sen, poverty is synonymous with suffering from an entitlement failure or a denial of rights. The issue of rights and entitlements raises issues around power or powerlessness which also has become recognised as a central component of poverty.

Accordingly, poverty is a 'lack of voice,' or influence within the socio-political sphere. Other rights-based definitions stress that poverty manifests itself as a denial of the rights to personal dignity, autonomy, and social inclusion, of the right to equality between social groups, and of the right to political freedom and security. Returning to a more material-based definition of poverty, empirical research points out that poverty can be both chronic and transient.

In the latter case, changing economic circumstances (which may in turn be connected to political or environmental factors) push some people 'in and out of poverty.' In other words, during certain periods some people may become poor, and also more poor, but at other times the same people may be relatively affluent. Hence, vulnerability to changing circumstances and susceptibility to deprivation of basic needs, material assets, and/or income/consumption is therefore another dimension of poverty.

Although certain dimensions of poverty may prevail in particular temporal and geo-political contexts, generally it is more useful to view poverty as a complex phenomenon that often includes some or all of the above dimensions. Moreover, it is worth noting that the defining characteristics of poverty also are invoked as its causes (e.g., a persistent lack of income or material assets might be declared the cause, as well as the symptom, of poverty).

The causes can constitute a set of interlocking vicious cycles, for example, illness may prevent someone from working, leading to a decline in income, which may in turn result in the inability to procure enough food or medicine, leading to a further decline in health. This may necessitate the sale of material assets in order to obtain the, thereby increasing individual vulnerability to changing economic circumstances while also leading to a decline in socio-economic status and influence in the community, etc.

Thus, poverty must be viewed as a process as well as a phenomenon. Finally, poverty may be defined both objectively (absolute) and subjectively (relative). The international poverty line is based on an absolute definition of poverty. Subjective/relative definitions determine poverty in comparison to other groups within a given society. Strategies that rely on absolute/objective definitions aim to raise the standard of living of all people to a common minimum standard. Strategies that rely on relative/subjective definitions aim to reduce societal inequalities.

All of these definitions of poverty however, are constructed, usually by those who are not poor, and imposed on 'poor' groups. The terminology used to categorise countries is always problematic, if only because it ignores the fine gradations between them. The terminology is also loaded with political, historical, and ideological baggage.

Tourism refers to those industries that provide accommodation, transportation and other services (e.g. the sale of souvenirs and other goods, restaurants, guided tours, etc.) for visitors who come from outside the destination for a period of more than 24 hours and less than one year. The visitors are commonly known as tourists. Visitors who spend less than 24 hours in the destination area are 'same-day visitors'.

Tourism and tourists can be subdivided into three categories. Domestic tourists reside within the destination country; regional tourists come to the destination country from distinct yet neighbouring countries (i.e., from the same continent or sub-continent). While regional tourists are in fact 'international', in this study the term international tourist applies primarily to visitors who come from other continents.

The WTO claims that the motivation for (domestic) tourist travel might include a) leisure, recreation and holidays, b) visiting friends and relatives; c) business and professional; d) health treatment; e) religion/pilgrimages;

and f, other'. Mass or mainstream tourism is oriented toward large package tours and luxury hotels, while niche tourism in theory involves more specialised markets (e.g., adventure travel, cultural tours, ecotourism, etc.), smaller groups, and often 'simpler' accommodation.

The latter is ostensibly more culturally and environmentally sensitive. Features of the niche, however, have also become incorporated into mass tourism operations. For example, package tours offered by luxury hotels sometimes include safari trips, treks and 'cultural visits.' Large numbers of people now participate in supposed alternatives to mass tourism, and numerous mainstream operators have adopted 'green' and 'eco' labels.

It is therefore questionable whether ecotourism and other forms of niche tourism are truly more environmentally and culturally sensitive than mass tourism. Every type of tourism that has proliferated in the last two decades, it is worth drawing attention to specific areas within the industry that have been particularly promoted by donors and NGOs:

— *Green tourism*: making the industry more environmentally sound by addressing problems of energy use and waste disposal

— *Nature-based tourism/ecotourism*: small-scale tourism that often occurs in or around conservation areas and which has as its primary objective the preservation of the environment

— *Heritage tourism*: tourism in historic areas that fund the preservation and restoration of buildings and monuments

— *Community-based tourism*: tends to be initiated or directed by local communities, or individuals within those communities, often to further community interests.

These four areas often converge under the umbrella of 'sustainable tourism.' While sustainable tourism and community-based tourism have in certain cases benefited poor people and they do contain key principles of PPT, they are not identical.

Pro-poor tourism

Even though sustainable tourism projects increasingly seek to address economic, social and cultural concerns, the rhetoric of sustainable tourism focuses on protection and conservation. While local populations must reap some social or economic benefits from tourism, this is principally to assure their cooperation and support for the primary objective of conservation; the benefits that accrue to local populations are a bonus.

'In contrast, pro-poor tourism aims to expand opportunities. Net benefits to the poor is a goal in itself, to which environmental concerns should contribute'. Although some community-based tourism enterprises have key objectives that go beyond conservation of natural environments and cultural heritage, PPT requires more than a community focus. According to DFID 'Pro-poor tourism generates net benefits for the poor (i.e. benefits are greater than costs).

Economic benefits are only one (very important) component - social, environmental and cultural costs and benefits also need to be taken into account. Pro-poor tourism strategies are concerned specifically with impacts on poor people, though the non-poor may also benefit. Strategies focus less on expanding the overall size of tourism, and more on unlocking opportunities for specific groups within it (on tilting the cake, not expanding it)'.

PPT is not restricted to community-based enterprises or to a particular segment of the industry, whether niche or mass. Ultimately, PPT consists of a set of principles rather than a distinct form of tourism. PPT initiatives represent practical steps that can transform strategies and principles into concrete action. For example, the enhancement of economic opportunities for the poor in tourism is one example of a PPT strategy.

An organisation attempting to operationalise that strategy at the destination level might provide employment or casual labour to the poor, it could establish supply linkages with poor merchants or farmers and outsource some services (e.g., laundry), training programmes, or joint ventures with communities, among other options. These practical efforts are a few of the more obvious examples of PPT initiatives.

The role of government may also be significant in enhancing or protecting poor peoples' access to tourism markets through different policy instruments. These could include making it compulsory to use local guides, establishing and enforcing ethical codes for labour and trade practices as well as zoning regulations, and promoting ethical consumption via public awareness campaigns. Yet in order to maximise tourism's pro-poor potential, we must draw on lessons from current thinking on poverty reduction.

Poverty reduction through tourism

Successful poverty reduction efforts require complementary action at different levels - macro, meso, and micro levels, including:

— *enabling actions*: structural reforms that facilitate poverty reduction (e.g., to promote private sector enterprises and participation);

— *indirect/inclusive actions*: general sectoral support (e.g., in education, health, infrastructure, agriculture, etc.) which may benefit the poor without targeting them directly;

— *direct/focused actions*: to remedy particular problems experienced by poor people (e.g., by helping to develop skills, education, increase productivity by facilitating access to land and microcredit, implementing specific infrastructure projects like water supply and sanitation, supporting women's initiatives, etc.).

Since the causes and manifestations of poverty are multidimensional, numerous theories and approaches influence practical efforts to reduce poverty. Some theories (e.g., neoliberalism) stress the material dimensions of poverty and place emphasis on the role that economic factors play in poverty reduction, while others highlight the salience of socio-political factors (e.g., governance and civil society approaches).

Yet due to tourism's potential to contribute to poverty reduction first and foremost in economic terms, the following theoretical overview will concentrate on perspectives that directly address the economic and livelihood implications of the industry for the poor.

These perspectives include neoliberalism and its critics at the macro-level, and the sustainable livelihoods framework at the micro-level.

Many analysts agree that economic growth is crucial to poverty reduction. Neoliberal assumptions have guided the growth-based poverty reduction strategies of aid agencies in the industrial countries and multilateral development banks. Neoliberalism is based on the premise that free interaction between individuals as economic agents will maximise the welfare of the greatest numbers in the global population.

Accordingly, free market exchange patterns are self-correcting, and the benefits of growth in certain sectors of society will ultimately 'trickle down' to other sectors. Outward-oriented growth (i.e., export-oriented) based on 'comparative advantages' will stimulate growth most rapidly in developing countries which should in turn theoretically lead to faster poverty reduction. The following are the key principles of outward-oriented neoliberal growth strategies:

— Given low levels of domestic demand in many developing countries, growth in a range of economic sectors is largely dependent on gaining access to global markets via outward-oriented strategies.

— Outward-oriented policies are regarded as the least damaging in terms of micro-economic efficiency: they benefit total factor productivity more than any other popular policy option.

— Multiplier effects associated with foreign trade and tourism may facilitate long-term growth by expanding overall production and employment.

— Earnings from trade and tourism may foster macroeconomic stability by contributing to a more favourable balance of payments. This is important for attaining good ratings in international financial markets, and thus access to foreign loans and other investment capital.

— Such earnings may also provide foreign exchange for imported goods, particularly capital goods needed to increase the production potential of an economy.

— Rising volume in the external sector and increased competition within global markets are believed to create economic efficiencies associated with increasing scale economies and technological diffusion.

— Given these theoretical arguments, rapid economic growth among (especially) East Asian export-oriented New Industrialising Countries (NICs), as well as a series of country studies showing strong correlations between an outward-orientation and economic performance, is interpreted as empirical evidence supporting the externally-led growth hypothesis.

In order to maximise market efficiency, neoliberal institutions like the World Bank and the International Monetary Fund (IMF) have traditionally supported the restriction of government intervention to the removal of political obstacles that may distort 'natural' market exchange patterns. The curtailment of state responsibilities is one feature of the structural adjustment programmes (SAPs) that the IMF imposes in order to liberalise (i.e., to give free reign to the laws of supply and demand) the markets of developing countries that have taken conditional loans.

As a poverty reduction strategy, the conventional neoliberal model has its flaws, and institutions like the World Bank now acknowledge that rapid economic growth alone is insufficient to eliminate poverty. In the World Development Report 2000/2001, the World Bank notes that:

'Market reforms can be central in expanding opportunities for poor people, but reforms need to reflect local institutional and structural conditions. And mechanisms need to be in place to create new opportunities and compensate the potential losers in transitions. In societies with high inequality, greater equity is particularly important for rapid progress in reducing poverty. This requires action by the state to support the buildup of human, land, and infrastructure assets that poor people own or to which they have access.'

The Bank now considers that political empowerment of the poor (through increased accountability of state and public institutions, greater participation of the poor in decision making processes, etc.).and the enhancement of security (reducing the vulnerability of the poor to economic disasters, crises, and risks) must occur simultaneously for growth to maximise poverty reducing opportunities.

Significantly, several definitions of broad-based growth exist, not all of which are concerned with maximising the welfare of the poor. The World Bank's notion of broad-based growth is among the most widely accepted.

In addition, pro-poor growth depends on an existing equitable distribution of assets, especially in terms of land and human capital. Governments usually promote tourism on the basis of its potential to contribute to macro-economic growth and job creation. Up to now, few governments (or private companies) have linked tourism development directly to poverty reduction efforts.

As a highly sophisticated sector, strongly influenced by marketing skills, information technology and a few large Northern-based companies, tourism may seem an inappropriate sector to start in shaping pro-poor growth. However, as tourism is rapidly growing in many developing countries, takes place in some poor and isolated areas, and is relatively labour intensive, it is important to assess whether and how pro-poor principles can be adopted within the sector.

While tourism in itself is insufficient as a poverty reduction strategy, it could be a significant component of a broader pro-poor economic growth strategy. Still, critics point out that the structure of the industry and the international political economy minimise the potential economic benefits that most developing countries and the poor can obtain from tourism.

The sustainable livelihoods approach which has emerged over the course of the last decade or so, stresses the need for local participation and a 'fit' between strategies, the existing livelihoods of the poor, builds on poor people's assets and environmental limitations. Thus, for tourism to become an effective poverty reduction strategy, it should complement the existing livelihoods of the poor by providing an opportunity for economic diversification without disrupting or substituting those livelihoods.

If the costs to the poor (whether economic, social, or environmental) of participation in tourism should outweigh the benefits, then it is not an appropriate pro-poor strategy. The suitability of tourism as a pro-poor strategy evidently will vary by social and environmental context.

There are four primary motivations drive tourism development:

— Private commercial gain

— Macro-economic growth objectives

— Environmental and/or cultural conservation

— Rural development

Commercial gain is probably the single most important objective underlying tourism development, and the private sector therefore is a leading force in the industry. Governments, especially those that have adopted neo-liberal economic policies, consider tourism a powerful engine of macro-economic growth and job creation, and therefore encourage the industry's development.

NGOs and some governments are increasingly pushing 'small scale' niche tourism (e.g., ecotourism and cultural tourism) as a means of funding environmental, wildlife, and cultural conservation projects. Finally, governments, NGOs, communities, and even international donors have recently begun to explore tourism's potential as a springboard for rural development and poverty reduction.

Tourism is an industry driven primarily by commercial interests. While this means there may be limits to its pro-poor potential, it does have a number of characteristics and advantages over other sectors. Considering the size of the industry and how it already affects millions of poor people, 'a marginal improvement could generate substantial benefits'.

Research on tourism in developing countries has mostly focused on the general economic, environmental and socio-cultural impacts of the industry. The industry has many potentially beneficial impacts, but in practice these have been frequently outweighed by the negative consequences for local populations.

Up to now, governments and aid agencies have promoted enclave-oriented mass tourism due to its perceived macro-economic benefits. Due to the lack of communication between foreign dominated tourism enclaves and other sectors in the local economy, the multiplier effects of the industry are frequently lower than anticipated. The tourism industry is also accused of reinforcing 'longstanding (neo)colonial patterns of socio-economic and spatial polarisation'.

Evidently, the spatial polarisation of the tourism industry in many developing countries, the limited multiplier effects, and the lack of linkages with other economic sectors are more than macro-level.problems. Indeed, they manifest themselves at the micro level as restricted opportunities for the poor.

Mass tourism enclaves likewise receive a great deal of criticism for their unsound environmental practices and for the contempt many of their clients hold toward local cultural norms. The SAPs imposed by the IMF on many developing countries have created an uneven playing field on which domestic tourism enterprises in developing countries are at a disadvantage compared to foreign businesses and especially transnational corporations.

In order to meet the exigencies of SAPs, many developing countries 'have to direct their economy towards exporting goods and services, devalue their currency, cut down public expenditure in health and education, and privatise government-owned enterprises'. Those conditions have impeded local peoples in many developing countries from obtaining the skills and capital required to compete effectively with TNCs.

Moreover, developing countries with SAPs are pressured by multilateral institutions to liberalise their economies, thereby granting TNCs with greater expertise and capital the same rights to domestic markets that 'weaker' local entrepreneurs have. In some countries, 'over-liberalisation' of the tourism industry has impacted negatively on communities.

According to a study by Soraya Altorki of the American University in Cairo (AUC) explores the effects of tourism development on Marsa Matruh, a town which has expanded threefold in 30 years largely as a result of tourism. Its population is 35,000 people, with 54 hotels. This study suggests that any benefits from tourism, such as increased employment, construction and the like, have been overshadowed by the problems of increased imports, agricultural decline, the emergence of tourist 'enclaves', greater local resentment of tourists, and social problems such as alcoholism and the beginnings of a prostitution industry.

Understanding both the potential and pitfalls of tourism is a necessary first step towards making the industry more pro-poor. What is absent from most micro-level analyses, however, is a comparison of the various positive and negative impacts that tourism may have in a particular location and how they relate to the specific livelihood objectives of the local population. It is one thing to identify 'positive impacts'; it is another to consider how they fit with the livelihoods of the poor, according to PPT principles.

The distribution of both positive and negative tourism impacts varies across social groups. While generalisations are difficult to make due to the particularities associated with each tourism site, a few words concerning the effects of tourism on women and on the poor in developing countries are warranted.

Rapid tourism development and non-local investment tend to marginalise some segments of local communities by exacerbating the inequalities between the poor and those who have more capital. When the poor benefit from tourism, it is usually as street vendors or casual labourers (e.g., porters or 'low level' assistants in hotels, lodges, and tour organisations). Concerning the role of women in tourism, Shah and Gupta write that 'women find most opportunities in the informal sector, with activities ranging from collection and sale of firewood and carrying loads from road-heads, to shops and teashops [and handicrafts] and managing guesthouses in their own right'.

Several types of actors are involved in tourism. The term 'actor' refers to types of organisations distinguished according to their stake in tourism. The following are the actors:

— *Private sector companies:* These are formal commercial enterprises which operate independently of the state. Along with consumers, they are arguably the driving force of the tourism industry. While the vast majority of private companies are motivated by profit and commercial gain, in some cases they operate on a non-profit basis.

— *National, regional and local governments:* These include the official authorities governing a country or parts thereof. The category also includes various government departments at different levels who may have conflicting objectives (e.g., a national, regional or local tourist board and national parks and resources authority). National governments frequently promote tourism as a macro-economic growth strategy (micro-economic for local governments). In certain cases governments also include tourism in environmental and/or cultural conservation efforts, as well as in strategies for rural development.

— *International donors:* This is a large category that includes institutions like the World Bank, the United Nations, and the foreign aid agencies of the industrial countries, among others. Some qualify as international government organisations, some as transnational government organisations, and others as parastatals. While they have diverse objectives, these institutions tend to provide financial or other forms of support to tourism development without profiting from these developments directly. Donors sometimes include tourism in broader Third World development strategies, most commonly for macro-economic growth objectives, but increasingly also for environmental/wildlife conservation and rural development. Tourism is seldom invoked by donors as a distinct strategy for poverty reduction, although many currently are reconsidering their positions on tourism support.

— *Local, national, and international NGOs:* These are formally recognised organisations that are in theory independent of both states and the private sector, that are a part of civil society, and.which tend to operate on a non-profit basis. A plethora of NGOs exists representing virtually every area of social concern (from environment, human rights, to AIDS awareness, etc.). Several NGOs use tourism primarily as a strategy for environmental/wildlife and/or cultural conservation, and/or poverty alleviation. Some operate at the local level and work very closely or even emerge out of the activities of communities, while others target the broader national and international spheres. For the purposes of this study, registered charities are considered NGOs.

— *Community groups:* Also known as community-based organisations (CBOs), for the purposes of this study community groups refer to a formal or informal association of residents from a particular geographic locale (e.g., one or more villages and possibly nearby areas). All the residents of a village may participate in a tourism venture, or involvement in tourism may be limited to a subsection of the residents.

5

Tourism and Gender Development

The tourism sector definitely provides various entry points for women's employment and opportunities for creating self-employment in small and medium sized income generating activities, thus creating paths towards the elimination of poverty of women and local communities in developing countries.

However, there are a number of conditions under which this potential can be used more effectively. This requires collaboration of all stakeholders - governments and intergovernmental bodies, local government, industry, trade unions, local communities and their different member groups, NGOs, community based tourism initiatives, etc. Increasing the use of tourism's potential whilst safeguarding the natural environment and cultural heritage and increasing social and economic justice should be the goal of further tourism development. The aims at contributing to this goal.

Poverty Elimination through Tourism Development

In the last few decades, the tourism industry has undergone a period of explosive growth, and as a labour intensive industry, there has consequently been a rapid rate of job creation and development. Using the latest available data from the restaurant and hotel sector, provided by ILO and UNDP, examined the industry on a global level in terms of the numbers of women in employment over the past ten years, their average weekly wage rate and hours of work, as compared to men.

We have used the "restaurant, catering and hotel industry" to provide a proxy for the "tourism industry"; these sectors are the largest employers in the tourism industry overall. Gender disaggregated data for the tourism sector was not available for all countries. While data on numbers of women and men working in tourism related professions are more comprehensive than for the average wage and working hours; the availability of this information is still highly limited.

The general picture suggests that the tourism industry seems to be a particularly important sector for women as their percentages of employment in most countries are higher than in the workforce in general. The numbers of women and their percentage of the workforce in tourism vary greatly between countries - from 2 % up to over 80 %.

Although there were few obvious regional trends it would appear that in those countries where tourism is a more mature industry women generally account for around 50 % of the workforce. Of the data available for the years between 1988 and 1997, it appears that there has been a broad increase in the participation of women for tourism industry at a global level.

The majority of this increase in female participation may be driven by the growth in the industry for specific countries, such as Puerto Rico, Chile and Turkey. For the industrially developed countries, there has been little change in the actual participation of women in the tourism industry.

The proportion of women's to men's working hours, available for 39 countries, is 89 %—which means that women work 89 hours when men work 100 hours. The proportion of women's to men's wages is 79 %. At first glance, this looks like women are working less hours than men and at the same time receive even less pay. However, if this is due to women's typical occupations being paid less, women being significantly more in part time and/or temporary employment, and/or women being paid less for the same work (wage inequity).

In addition, readers should keep in mind that the increase of women's involvement in the labour market has not been associated with substantial change in the amount of hours women are expected to spend on domestic duties; this is leading to much longer actual working hours for women, ie up to 70-90 hours per week. Regarding the disproportionate relation between women's and men's working hours and their respective wages, there is a divide between the developed world, which employs females on an average weekly wage equivalent to 80% of a male's wage, and the less developed world, where average female wages fall by another 10% to 70% of male wages.

However, there are significant variations within these groups. Finally, readers should be aware that the data do not include information about the informal sector. This leaves us with a skewed picture as the informal sector plays a very important role in terms of income generation through tourism, particularly for women.

Women's occupations

Some facts about women's positioning in terms of hierarchical levels have been extracted from the very few sources giving information, which is not sufficiently differentiated. However, it seems very clear that the situation in the tourism industry resembles the one in the labour markets in general: As in many other sectors, there is a significant horizontal and vertical gender segregation of the labour market in tourism.

Horizontally, women and men are placed in different occupations - women are being employed as waitresses, chambermaids, cleaners, travel agencies sales persons, flight attendants, etc., whereas men are being employed as barmen, gardeners, construction workers, drivers, pilots, etc. Vertically, the typical "gender pyramid" is prevalent in the tourism sector - lower levels and occupations with few career development opportunities being dominated by women and key managerial positions being dominated by men.

Examining the occupations being particularly relevant in the tourism sector, one can see that more than 90 % of people working in catering & lodging, as waitresses, bartenders, maids, babysitters, cleaners, housekeeping helpers, launderers, dry-cleaners, and the like, are women.

Vertical segregation of the labour market in the service and the administrative / managerial sectors reflects the situation in the labour markets in general. Women around the world have achieved higher levels of education than ever before and today represent more than 40 % of the global workforce. Yet their share of management positions remains unacceptably low, with just a tiny proportion succeeding in breaking through the "glass ceiling".

There are numerous inter-linked factors, which help to maintain gender segregation of the labour market. Among them are gender stereotyping, traditional gender roles and gender identity - women are seen as being suitable for certain occupations and they seem themselves as suitable. In addition, traditional gender roles assign to women the main responsibilities for raising children, caring for the elderly, and doing household work.

Thus, women are often forced to choose casual labour, part-time and seasonal employment. Women are much more likely to be employed on a part time basis than men are. Although this allows them to accommodate the various responsibilities plus their work outside the home, it does have significant drawbacks: in many cases lower pay per working hour, fewer advancement opportunities, less formal training, less protection from unemployment, etc.

Acknowledging that the problem of gender segregation of labour markets is a general one should not mean that it isn't addressed when discussing tourism. Bringing the necessary changes about requires efforts in all sectors. However, the tourism industry seems to be a particularly good "candidate" for engaging in efforts towards the advancement of women. Due to its size, its rapid growth and its extremely diverse and dynamic nature, the tourism industry has an enormous flexibility.

This can enable the industry to develop key initiatives for the advancement of women so that other industries can benefit from initiatives and strategies in the tourism sector as models for their own development. The high percentage of women in the tourism workforce in many countries provides a necessary fundament for the further advancement of women: The "critical mass" is already there.

Community based tourism initiatives, particular of local women's groups and co-operatives, can be an accessible and suitable entry point for women into the paid workforce. They seem to generate more longterm motivation than initiatives from outside. There are numerous examples where women and women's groups have started income generating activities on their own.

These activities help to create financial independence for local women and challenge them to develop the necessary skills and improve their education. Research has shown that financial independence and good education lead to improved selfesteem of women and more equitable relationships in families and communities. Marketing seems to be a key constraint for the expansion of community based tourism. Independent initiatives need more information about markets and potential customers.

Tourists need to be provided with more information about the benefits of buying locally and using local services. Creating opportunities for income generating activities as well as effective marketing depend upon access to information about tourism related planning and decision-making in a community area.

Access to information is provided at best by involving all stakeholders in planning and decision-making. In addition, gender specific information about tourists' needs and interests helps to serve women customers. Many of the community based tourism initiatives studing depend upon the conservation of natural resources, protected areas and national parks around which they arose.

Therefore, pro-active protection of natural resources in tourism destinations is needed to sustain the basis of the livelihoods of community members being involved in tourism activities. The same applies to the conservation of local cultures and cultural heritage sites, which forms the basis of many tourism activities.

Another common aspect is the seasonal nature of tourism industry. Some argue that this creates a particularly good condition for women enabling them to accommodate their various responsibilities. However, this should not be seen as a general rule. In many cases, women and mothers cannot rely on a regular income forming the basis of the household income but have themselves to generate income all year.

Education and training

In many new destinations of the South, the local population faces a disadvantage for gaining entry into the formal sector because of low levels of education. The case studies indicate that there is a significant demand for education and training in the communities in and around popular destinations. Training, especially training for self-employment, has been an important element for success.

Most training activities are easy to replicate and could thus become an important part of an action strategy for the future. There is little evidence of training to enable or improve participation in the formal sector.

These are among the most prominent reasons why women and men tend to pursue different occupations and horizontal and vertical segregation of labour markets prevails. Gender stereotypes are prevalent in most cultures and rather resemble each other than being culturally specific.

Gender stereotypes influence the way perceive each other and how see ourselves. Women are perceived as being particularly suited to fill certain positions in tourism, they tend to see themselves as suited and tend to be interested in stereotypical occupations. Thus, women are in fact particularly suited to take on certain jobs, for example involving caring and household-related work and service positions.

On the one hand, this serves to perpetuate gender stereotyping and positioning of women accordingly. This is not generally desirable, particularly because most gender stereotypical occupations are lower paid and do not include key managerial positions.

On the other hand, the situation allows women to enter the tourism workforce based on their traditional roles and their own confidence to fulfil them. Addressing the issue of gender stereotypes and gender roles is not tourism-specific; rather it seems that the tourism sector is yet another example where traditional stereotypes and roles come into play. However, tourism could play a key role in challenging gender stereotypes.

Planning and Management

Tourism, especially international tourism that involves high capital investments, has tended to be controlled by powerful vested interests and has been characterised by a lack of concern for the local communities residing in the destination areas. In many areas the local communities or sections of local communities have taken the initiative to maximise gains for themselves.

In most cases this has been a spontaneous development. However, there have been attempts to introduce systematic processes or strategies to enhance participation by all sections of the host communities, with several of these having a gender focus. There have also been attempts to build up partnerships, partnerships between the formal tourist industry and local communities and partnerships between concerned government departments, NGOs and local communities. It is just a beginning. The experience gained, however, can provide the building blocks for scaling up and evolving effective strategies at various levels, local, national, regional and international.

Apart from developing good governance, income generation is the important motive for participation by women in the tourism industry. In most destination areas in the South, the gains for the local community seem to come from the informal sector or the formal sector owned or organised by the communities. Coming out very strongly in the case studies is the conclusion that the community must be involved in all stages of tourism development—be it the engagement of tourism industry coming in from outside, community based tourism initiatives, or a combination of those.

Capacity building for participation is needed in many cases. It is important to acknowledge that different groups have different requirements in terms of capacity building and empowerment; in particular women and men. There are several examples of building partnerships contained in the found elsewhere.

Promotion of community participation in the tourism industry forms an important part of the evolving trend. External interventions, especially designed and funded by multilateral and bilateral agencies played a significant role in the development of this trend. Several cases help in understanding the role of conservation departments as stakeholders in participatory tourism development.

Tourism boards and government departments dealing with tourism do not seem to be playing a very active role in promoting the participation of local communities as stakeholders or in facilitating partnerships between the local communities and the tourist industry. Some cases show how NGOs can play the role of social entrepreneurs in the industry. In many areas tourism seems to have the potential for reducing the dependencies of NGOs on external funding.

Tourist participation in conservation has proved to be a success. This could be extended to cover areas such as infrastructure development, health and education. This approach could also be used to develop new concepts of tourism itself.

Women's Rights

The United Nations Convention on the Elimination of all Forms of Discrimination Against Women and the

Universal Declaration of Human Rights must form the basis of addressing human rights and women's rights issues in tourism. Women can suffer specific discrimination within the tourism sector. Women are consistently denied positions of leadership and responsibility within the industry, they are concentrated in low skilled and low paid occupations, they are being objectified as part of the tourism "package" and they can have their traditional roles perpetuated within an industry that feeds on uncomplicated images.

Tourism can violate women's rights, but it can also be used to challenge traditional roles and to empower women, in economic, social, cultural and political terms. The case studies show that women can find a voice and independence through getting involved in tourism activities - by becoming part of decision-making processes and carving out new roles in their families, homes and within local power structures.

With sex tourism being the most negative and prominent example, there is a significant amount of sexual objectification of women working in the tourism industry. Studies have shown that women are expected to dress in an "attractive" manner, to look beautiful (ie slim, young, pretty) and to 'play along' with sexual harassment by customers. Stereotypical images of women are in many cases part of the tourism product. Friendly smiling women, fitting certain standards of attractiveness, who seem to be waiting to submissively serve the customer's every wish are being portrayed. Women working at destinations as well as indigenous women are being shown in a stereotypical way in tourism brochures and other material.

As women are not only confronted with the challenges of setting up income generating activities but often also with the challenges of altering their traditional roles in their communities by generating independent income, becoming a 'leader' or a 'business woman', there is an understandable need for mutual support and exchange of strategies how to meet these challenges.

Linkages between the tourist industry and other sectors of the economy and the creation of indirect employment is another under-researched area. This would allow for more targeted approaches to creating income-earning opportunities to those who are not directly involved in tourism through backward and forward linkages. Maximising benefits for local communities must address the problem of financial leakages. There is a need to assess leakages and to promote good practice strategies to minimise them.

As in many other areas, lack precise data on women's and men's employment in the tourism industry - their occupations, positioning in the hierarchies, contracts, wages, working hours, training, etc. Few countries provide information about these variables; in some cases, they are available through the tourism industry.

Identifying the most gender-responsive aspects of tourism development: Participatory processes and setting up community based tourism initiatives benefit greatly from having information available about which areas of planning and management most urgently need women's participation.

Intergovernmental bodies as well as governments can play a vital role in minimising the impacts of natural disasters on tourism National, regional and international networking among women being involved in tourism activities should be built up more effectively and widespread.

Labour Market Opportunities in Tourism Industry

Worldwide, ecotourism is the fastest growing segment of the tourism industry, increasing at a rate of 4 - 10% annually. The Toronto region is a gateway to tourism in Canada, with a record 28.0 million people passing through the Pearson International Airport in 2001. Departures and arrivals at the airport are expected to grow by over 40% to at least 50 million by 2020.

Urban green tourism brings ecotourism to the city, taking advantage of emerging consumer trends and shifting demographics, and capitalizing on the efficiencies of the urban form to advance sustainable development goals and to support and enhance the quality of life and local economies of our urban regions.

Toronto's Green Tourism Association (GTA) has been working since 1996 to promote and develop urban green tourism in the Toronto region. Its mission is: "-to develop and cultivate a green tourism industry within the Toronto region. An industry that is ecologically sound, fosters appreciation of and respect for diverse cultural and natural heritages, and strengthens local economies and communities."

In 1996 The GTA commissioned Blackstone Corporation to undertake a feasibility study on the potential for urban green tourism in Toronto. It concluded: "Emerging tourism trends and opportunities and gaps identified by the primary tourism documents of the 1990's suggest that the Partnership's goals are timely, ideally positioned to capitalize on emerging market trends, and hold the potential to generate cultural, environmental and economic benefits.

Toronto will have lost an opportunity to strengthen its long-term competitiveness and may risk losing market share to other destinations that do cater to the needs and preferences of the, new tourist for variety, environmental soundness, authenticity and novelty."

Research showed that over the last decade, the nature of the tourism industry has shifted in response to key market drivers which include, but are not limited to:

— Increasing demand for urban green tourism-related services and products, spurred by environmental and social awareness and concern amongst urban consumers about growing congestion, smog, and other environmental and social issues;

— Increasing supply of new urban green tourism services, products, technologies, knowledge, and skills; and

— New tourism trends and approaches, including ecotourism, sustainable tourism, urban tourism, and responsible tourism, all related to emerging cultural preferences and demographic shifts..

Urban green tourism development is in keeping with universal urban and new economy trends including:

— Increased concern about quality of urban life, environment, and economy;

— Rapid population growth in cities including an increasing seniors' population;

— Increasingly urbanized and flexible lifestyles;

— Increased access to new technologies which facilitate mobility and information exchange;

— Sustainable development priorities in municipalities, and

— Increased domestic travel following September 11, 2001.

There is an awareness amongst related industry representatives of general urban green tourism principles, however, there is as yet little identification of or with urban green tourism and its cross-cutting aspects as a cohesive industry sector. More, and more in-depth research is required to fill information gaps related to urban green tourism, in particular with regard to human resource gaps and opportunities.

There are identified areas of opportunity and employment growth related to urban green tourism, including: tour operation (packaging, guiding); environmental tourism; education and training; research and marketing; business development; sustainable transportation and new mobility; and resource management.

There are identified knowledge and skill requirements related to urban green tourism including:

— environmental tourism skills;

— human and interpersonal skills;

— business and management skills;

— integrative and brokering skills; and

— cultural and environmental knowledge and skills.

There are identified barriers to employment related to urban green tourism, including:

— lack of sufficient financing for, and investment in, urban green tourism initiatives and directions;

— lack of awareness of urban green tourism and its diverse and significant potential;

— lack of urban green tourism infrastructure and social, policy, and academic supports;

— lack of leadership in urban green tourism amongst all sectors; and

— lack of education and training related to urban green tourism.

Promote better understanding and awareness of the evolving urban green tourism industry and its labour market opportunities by all stakeholders within and across sectors. Promote capacity building, innovation, and leadership amongst the diverse players in the evolving industry in relation to urban green tourism and its labour market and employment opportunit ies.

Using online tools and networking events, establish a foundation for linking the key players in urban green tourism on an ongoing basis, both within particular industries and initiatives, and across the range of industries and initiatives related to urban green tourism. Online Tools Building on existing efforts and infrastructure, establish an urban green tourism web network or portal, providing easy access and links to:

— Industry Trends (news and reports);

— Best Practices (searchable and self-publishing);

— Online interactive networks across the industry

(directories of key players, initiatives, and groups, chat rooms, videoconferencing by topic and industry sector); and

— Employment, mentorship and co-op exchange opportunities involving employers, potential employees, and academic institutions.

Host and participate in conferences, workshops, career fairs, and other networking opportunities related to urban green tourism human resources development. In partnership with appropriate business, government, labour, academe, and community representatives, support and/or undertake educational and professional development initiatives aimed at building capacity related to urban green tourism knowledge, skills and training.

Such initiatives may include, but are not limited to: Curriculum development for colleges, universities, and schools, covering environmental tourism skills, communication and interpersonal skills, business management skills, teaching and integrative skills, and history, culture, heritage, and environmental knowledge related to urban green tourism. In many cases theses various topics could be integrated, and course offerings could be cross-listed through co-operative multi-institutional arrangements.

Professional development courses aimed at providing knowledge and skills to employees and potential employees in industries and occupations related to urban green tourism, to provide relevant and practical knowledge and skills related to urban green tourism. Identify policies that enable and enhance as well as challenge or deter urban green tourism human resources development. Such policies may relate to tourism, economic development, finance and taxation, land use and transportation, social equity and diversity, parks and heritage, culture, and human resources development.

6

Human Resource Management

The traditional constraints of the hotel, catering and tourism industry - long, antisocial working hours, low pay, unstable, seasonal employment, low job status, etc. - make employment within the industry appear unattractive to many. A study carried out in 1996 in Germany found that employment in the hotel and catering trade was not the first choice for nine out of ten employees, while only one employee in seven was satisfied with the trade as a choice of career.

Nevertheless, the industry does attract some people either on a short-term basis or for a long-term career. The immediate and most obvious consequences of such a situation are the difficulty of recruiting suitable staff and high staff turnover; both these effects are costly to the industry. There is therefore a perceived need for human resource development, to raise the profile of the industry, increase productivity and provide decent, sustainable employment within the sector.

A wide range of technological developments in service in hotels may be affecting productivity. Integrated management systems are enabling hotel companies to computerize day-to-day reception operations. Clients are thus able to make their own reservations via the Internet, while electronic in-room installations make it possible to settle accounts from the hotel room.

This technology will also make it possible to monitor the productivity of personnel, while new techniques in food preparation and storage are reducing the skills needed in the kitchen and the time required for food preparation. Hotels are therefore seeking new ways to measure service delivery that take into account customer satisfaction and return visits, rather than sticking to a narrow "input/output" system.

In Europe, tourist-related activities account on average for 5.5 per cent of GDP in all European Union Member States and for a total of 9 million employees, representing 6 per cent of the total workforce. The precise percentages vary from country to country. According to WTTC simulated figures, the tourism industry's labour force represents about 3 per cent of the world's total labour force and produces about 4 per cent of total world GDP. The industry can therefore not be regarded as labour intensive throughout.

In the hotel industry in developing countries there may be on average up to three people employed for each hotel bed, while in developed countries the inverse is true, with one person employed for up to three or even four hotel beds. However, figures of this sort can be affected by the range of services provided by a hotel: an establishment surrounded by a leisure complex, health resort or spa will naturally employ more ancillary workers.

Labour productivity in hotels has increased over the last ten years by about 1 per cent per year. In the United States, the number of employees per 100 hotel rooms sold has declined from 81 in 1986 to 75 in 1997. The same productivity growth applies to the entire HCT sector whose GDP, according to WTTC simulated figures, has been growing by about 3 per cent per year, whilst employment in the industry has grown by only about 2 per cent per year.

Labour productivity in restaurants is hard to measure. Since only 50-60 per cent of all restaurant employees worldwide are full-time workers, the information available hardly allows us to establish absolute productivity ratios. The First World Travel and Tourism Summit, held in 1977 in Vilamoura, Portugal, recognized that travel and tourism create an unparalleled number of entry-level jobs for young people and women and provides part-time or seasonal employment for people seeking flexible working arrangements.

The Summit called for the reduction of rigid practices in labour markets to encourage greater staff mobility, productivity and innovation in a progressive employment environment, with emphasis on a flexible market economy, avoiding protectionist regulation. The Conclusions and Recommendations of the European Union's High Level Group on Tourism and Employment drew attention to the fact that notable adjustments were taking place in European tourism, that these were critical to its competitiveness, and that they would lead to important changes in the tourism labour market. Those are:

— a refocusing of core competencies;

— a deskilling of operational tasks in some sub-branches;

— upgrading of skills and specializations, in particular in large enterprises and tourist organizations and in complementary services; and

— the creation of new professional profiles to meet tourists' needs and preferences.

A positive example of flexibility is provided by the Sheraton-Denver West Hotel in the United States, where two experienced sales managers share one full-time job, thus enabling the company to benefit from the energy and experience of two persons for the price of one. In this instance, both managers wanted to work part time to accommodate their personal and family needs. The arrangement was particularly effective, since both managers were in continual contact.

Job-sharing opportunities of this kind will be even more viable in the future, as information becomes more comprehensively shared and more easily transmitted. One opportunity which has been insufficiently investigated is the possibility of using the inter-season period as a time for training to impart new skills, guaranteeing re-employment of qualified staff in successive seasons so as to retain their services.

A hotel located in Savonlinna (South-Savo, Finland), a city famous for its summer opera festivals, has adopted this approach. To deal with the multicultural and demanding clientele drawn by the summer festival, the hotel pays its core staff to attend off-season training courses in language skills, knowledge of food and wine and leadership skills. Employee development is seen not as a cost but as an investment which pays good returns during the summer season.

The employers argue that one way to create sustainable, realistic employment in the industry is to implement a policy of "multiskilling". This is also viewed as a means of reducing the problems of recruitment. Multiskilling has always been practised in small enterprises, but it is only recently that particular attention has been paid to it.

As demand for general competencies in small enterprises as well as in major hotel and restaurant chains has grown, and as appropriate means of training for these competencies have been developed, awareness has grown of the importance of multiskilling in that segment. One person fulfilling several roles at different times of the day combines the tasks of several (part-time) jobs into one job.

Multiskilling is also seen as a way to create or preserve a number of full-time jobs, as opposed to part-time jobs, since the tasks may be performed at any time of the day. Instead of employing specialists on a less than full-time basis, employees are trained to perform the tasks of several specialists, often supported by facilitating technology.

In Finland, a relatively small hotel has adopted a "multitask" policy. All its employees must be willing to perform any of the tasks that are necessary to operate the hotel. When hiring staff, the hotel manager gives precedence to "right personality" over all other criteria. Some workers left when this decision was taken which suggests that the approach is not universally appealing to employees.

Corporate organizations are downsizing and restructuring, which means that they are cutting back on layers of management. This means that less direction is being imparted to employees, who are more frequently required to accept a greater degree of responsibility and accountability. Increased use of technology in the workplace also means an added responsibility for individual workers. It is estimated that the "knowledge revolution", by providing clear information via the Internet on all the industry's tangible elements will make the intangible elements all the more important. Lower levels of staff will be empowered to act autonomously.

Command and control structures are thus largely giving way to a participatory teamwork approach. Human resources trained to fit in with new working methods will have to be regarded as an asset in which investment must be made, rather than merely as a cost, or employees will seek employment elsewhere. Management is developing ways in which to attract and retain employees.

The advent of new technology will not stop the industry from being a supplier of entry-level jobs; clearly, a large number of routine jobs will continue to exist. However, the question of staff retention will remain a management problem. Information technology will make potential entrants to the industry more aware of the possibilities available, compounding the problem for the industry. In order to retain staff, certain companies have already set up an incentive system.

McDonalds introduced a broad-based stock ownership programme in 1995 to improve staff morale and productivity, while in Europe, one major hotel chain has established the CHAMPS reward programme, in which employees earn points for cleanliness, hospitality, accuracy, product quality and speed. These points can be used to buy catalogue merchandise.

Truly structured careers, in which workers have genuine prospects of career development, are not numerous in the hotel, tourism and catering sector, and efforts to retain employees through incentives or promotion are the exception rather than the rule. Not only do people tend to "pass through" the sector, but research has shown that it is often the most talented who leave, since they are the most confident of finding other employment, while the less confident stay for fear of becoming unemployed.

However, for many young people the industry is an entry point to the world of work. It brings workers into direct contact with the public and can provide opportunities for travel. Moreover, for young people, the provision of food and lodging - a common practice in the industry - facilitates entry into active adult life. These factors combine to make tourism a major motor for the social and professional integration of the young.

With the advent of new technologies and an increasingly discerning public able to keep informed through the Internet, the hotel sector is being forced to widen its sphere of action beyond the traditional provision of food and accommodation. In the pursuit of improving the intangibles, major hotel chains are seeking to provide more services, both in response to customers' needs and in an effort to provide an "experience" rather than simple lodging.

For example, the French Accor Group has expanded into travel agency services, car hire, casinos and on-board train services, while other groups have established connections with sectors that are indirectly linked to tourism, such as insurance, travel articles and health and beauty services. The range of services now expected by customers naturally requires an upgrading of skills among front-desk staff, who will for the most part be required to administer these services.

This will call for motivated personnel with excellent social skills and an understanding of what people want. Advances in computer technology allow far more rapid and detailed generation of information on quality and economic performance. Hotel managers will thus be called on to react more quickly, to analyse situations and take appropriate decisions.

The wider range of services on offer will also call for greater marketing skills than were previously necessary. In large hotels and hotel chains this is resulting in the creation of posts which are new to the industry, but which already exist in other fields, such as budget analysis and management accounting expert, quality manager, yield manager, technical and computer services manager.

With greater emphasis being placed on environmental protection, there is also an increasing need for experts on the environmental impact and planning of tourism development. Similarly, greater concern over food safety is creating a growing need for food safety and health experts. As the hotel sphere increasingly includes services catering for customers' entertainment needs, sports and games specialists as well as specialized tour guides are opening up as careers in the tourism sector.

Women traditionally play an important role in the hotel, restaurant and tourism sector. However, their access to the higher levels of the corporate structure remains problematic. In the United States, a recent study found that less than half of all managerial posts in hotels were held by women, while further figures show that although between 1985 and 1995 the number of women in restaurant supervisory positions rose by 34 per cent to 260,000, or 68.9 per cent of all food-preparation and service-providing jobs, they held only 8 per cent of seats on the boards of directors of 100 of the largest restaurant chains.

Moreover, they represented only 4 per cent of the industry's highest ranking officers, and 4 per cent of its top earners. To an extent this is the result of friction between family and work responsibilities, especially given the prevailing long working hours in the food-service business.

The lower wages paid to women make it more feasible for them to take time off from work to look after family needs than for their husbands to do so. To help resolve this problem, enterprises are starting to introduce family-friendly programmes involving flexi-time, tele-commuting and childcare schemes. At the level of line employees, a United Kingdom hotel has found an innovative solution to problems it had been encountering in recruiting and retaining room service staff.

The hotel decided to target its recruitment efforts on mothers of school-age children and agreed to provide a play leader to look after the children during school holidays. The cost of the play leader was made up by saved advertising and recruitment costs previously incurred as a result of high staff turnover.

Nonetheless, it remains generally true that there is a gender-based income disparity across all segments of the hotel, catering and tourism industry. New divisions of labour and changes in the nature of jobs within the tourism sector mean that the industry is employing an increasingly varied range of employees. However, although tourism is a diverse sector which can provide many working opportunities for a wide range of skills, there is a shift within Europe away from specific skills towards broader, more generic competencies.

Good practice in training is largely limited to large hotel chains, and small, individual enterprises tend to rely on training given "on the job". According to research in Spain, managers of three-star hotels recognized that older workers rarely had any of the formal training required to deal with a more sophisticated clientele, and younger workers lacked industry-specific practical skills.

However, they were generally reluctant or unable to invest in training, on the grounds that the cost could not be sustained by their operations. The key training needs established by employers and trade unions are food safety, IT, environmental awareness and foreign language skills.

The industry provides few post-experience training or retraining opportunities, and, indeed, commitment by the private sector to human resource development appears slight, especially where such development lies beyond their immediate operational needs: "European companies, especially smaller businesses, provide little by way of financial and practical support for human resource development within the wider educational and training framework."

Within the multinational hotel industry, however, there is a trend towards investment in education, training and development, to meet the need for a higher level of customer-oriented service. The Radisson Hotel Group acknowledges that the success of the company depends on the knowledge, skills, abilities, motivation and dedication of its employees, and consequently has a well-developed internal training system, with links to outside training establishments as well, to which 0.4 per cent of each hotel's total revenue is dedicated.

In the United States in 1996, the Hospitality Business Alliance (HBA) was formed between the National Restaurant Association and the American Hotel and Motel Association to create a school-to-career programme. Worksite experience is an integral element of the training. During the school year, students work between 15 and 20 hours a week in the enterprise, gaining experience in front-desk operations, housekeeping, room service, safety and health, reservations, sales and marketing and convention services.

The system has grown from involving three high schools in 1997 to 600 high schools in 1999, covering 25 States and 11,000 students. One hotel group in the United Kingdom noted a training gap which was preventing the company's (multi-)unit managers, whose role is a largely implementational one, from progressing to a more strategic role within the enterprise.

The company's human resource department has organized strategic management development schemes at a number of leading business schools in the United Kingdom and the United States. The courses are designed to expose area managers to the strategic concepts of operational management, including corporate governance, finance, marketing and human resource strategy. This move to supply appropriate training is appreciated by unit managers aspiring to strategic, policy-creative posts.

A number of hotel chains have introduced schemes to enhance careers within their structures, with a view to reducing staff turnover. Choice Hotels International in the United States analysed the requirements for its senior executives on the basis of suitable existing competency models, then assessed the competencies of current top executives and compared these with the competencies needed for the future.

This enables the company to carry out annual readiness assessments and to establish a genuine career structure within the group, thus avoiding the disruption and expense of replacing executive staff. A further example is provided by Motel 6, which has established an HRD approach whereby every employee is eligible to become a manager, via a three-tier training scheme. By early 1998 this system had allowed around 300 Motel 6 employees to reach the grade of general managers, thereby helping to fill a need for qualified managers by providing employee training and the basis of a career structure.

An increasingly culturally diverse clientele has necessitated specialist training in the field of knowledge building for staff. ITT Sheraton operates a number of resort hotels in the Hawaiian islands, where the presence of Japanese clients has encouraged the creation of Japanese language and culture courses.

This initiative has resulted in a significant increase in the number of Japanese guests frequenting the hotels, while the courses themselves have become problem-solving sessions with staff. In 1992, the Four Seasons Hotel and Resort developed the Self-Access Learning Centre in Indonesia, where the company was opening a new resort, to teach English to locally recruited staff.

The courses were designed to take account of the fact that around 80 per cent of the staff had no more than primary-school education. The centre now teaches French and Japanese as well as Bahasa Indonesia. Employees are rewarded as they complete each of the five levels of the course with bonuses ranging from Rps.100,000 to Rps.250,000 (about $8-20), and a certificate of achievement.

Employees were invited to take on certain management duties: the front-office employees, for example, were invited to take over the role of the front-office manager. As an incentive, the hotel proposed dividing half of the savings obtained through the elimination of the post among the employees who had taken on the duties (about $1.00 each an hour). The replaced staff members were not sacked, but redistributed elsewhere in the company.

At another hotel, a system of self-directed housekeeping teams was established and responsibility given to the teams for choosing their own work areas, evaluating room quality and conducting room inspections; this has increased the staff retention rate and morale among room attendants. In 1993, Accor launched a three-year programme to "re-engineer" the structure of Sofitel North America.

The programme was designed to empower employees to make decisions to benefit guests, and called for volunteers eager to make improvements in services provided by the hotels. Since suggestions for improvements and alterations were now originating from the employees, peer resistance within each department was minimal: a culture of trust and communication was established.

The result has been an increase not only in customer satisfaction, but in employee satisfaction as well. Staff turnover fell from 58 per cent in 1993 to 39 per cent in

1998, below the industry average. Among the reasons frequently cited for reluctance to taking up employment in the hotel, tourism and catering trade, lack of promotion possibilities features prominently.

The broad pyramid of the hierarchy within the industry renders interpretation of the word "career" difficult. While careers are possible in the sector, and it is theorctically possible to progress from waiter to managing director of a major hotel chain, the increasingly flat management structures can only make this increasingly difficult.

On the other hand, systems designed to reward staff financially for their performance, with the aim of reducing staff turnover and encouraging a feeling of "belonging" to the enterprise, are not yet accepted by all staff, and vertical career aspirations are still widespread. Modern-minded employers trust that job satisfaction is tending to shift away from hierarchical feelings. Bonuses to enhance job satisfaction can be awarded (and sometimes withdrawn) at any time, according to individual or collective performance.

Tourism education and training

Employers maintain that many enterprises, especially SMEs, cannot pay wages commensurate with formal training and recognized qualifications. Others argue that the greater productivity made possible by training will make higher wages possible. In general, many of the operational activities in the industry require learning on the job, rather than formal training, and managers frequently state their preference for recruitment on the basis of personality rather than formal qualifications.

More than 60 per cent of operational staff in Germany and more than half the labour force in Austria have had no formal training. The industry displays a reluctance to give formal recognition to acquired skills, and this may reflect a wish to avoid claims for higher wages and prevent undesired mobility. On the other hand, a recent study also suggests that practical training and experience is more highly valued in the countries covered than formal, accredited training qualifications.

Moreover, high staff turnover in the industry makes returns on training investment hard to evaluate. Employees, who may not wish to develop a career in the industry or may be discouraged by poor scholastic performance, also avoid measurement by public standards. At middle management level and higher, however, tourism education is a formal requirement.

In Canada, more than one-third of jobs in hotels require post-secondary education, including language proficiency, but a Brazilian study shows that only 12 per cent of hotel and restaurant staff have completed secondary school. Tourism-related degree programmes have been slow to acquire recognition as a truly academic discipline although, given the increasing social and economic importance of tourism, a sound knowledge of its economic, social, cultural, environmental and political dimensions is essential.

This is particularly the case in countries, including developing countries, where tourism is growing rapidly. In Europe, tourism training is seen as a means of boosting employment and recouping Europe's dwindling market share in the industry.

In the Rhône-Alpes region of France, 7,000 new hotel and restaurant workers are required. Half the posts do not match formal training schemes. The bipartite committee on vocational training is therefore proposing that graduates acquire additional certificates to become waiters or wine-cellar specialists, as well as cooks, and is considering replacing the certification system with a system listing a variety of competencies.

Given the higher customer expectations of quality in a one-to-one relationship with the service personnel, an important part of the required skills concerns personal behaviour and communication, as opposed to specialized operational skills. The new skill requirements have an undeniable vertical element. The joint vocational training committee in Rhône-Alpes therefore recommends recruiting waiters with higher school qualifications.

However, workers with that level of education rarely seek employment as waiters. More complex workplaces have brought about a shift in training concerns from operational or vocational skills to personal and social skills. Operational skills are still required, but are increasingly focused on technological innovation. A capacity to learn and develop activities, and to assimilate all elements of a complex process, and effective communication skills, including negotiation in cases of conflict, are among the skills needed to enable today's worker to attain the necessary autonomy at work. This presents a challenge for training institutions geared towards operational skills, rather than "soft" skills.

New technical skills which need to be acquired by line-level employees include: deeper and more up-to-date knowledge of materials and production processes; knowledge of computer programs and other new technologies employed in kitchens and the concomitant new working methods; awareness of safety and health issues, an understanding of the house "business culture"; and an ability to impart an increasingly broad range of information to customers.

Language knowledge and a developed inter-cultural sensitivity are key skills for tourism personnel who have direct contact with customers. Management-level requirements mirror the qualities listed above, but also embrace a new approach to human resource management and development. Enterprises are espousing a philosophy by which workers receiving "good service" from their superiors are more likely to provide "good service" to customers.

Another important area of innovation and emphasis for management training is quicker response to - or anticipation of - market developments. This requirement is nothing new for top chain hotel managers, but it is new for many managers of smaller units and for department chiefs or supervisory-level managers. Adjusting in an autonomous way and developing innovative strategies require a capacity to generate the necessary flux of market information, and consequently also the ability to manipulate computer programmes.

This marks a significant departure from the traditional picture of the independent hotel manager as "a jack of all trades" who does not work within budgets or performance targets. Formally structured initial or primary training, including apprenticeships with practical and technical schooling, seems less adapted to the new "soft" skill requirements of today's industry than continuous training, and current thinking holds that it might be restricted to a minimal, multisector learning platform to raise the employability of young people and their mobility between different sectors.

Continuous training, which has the advantage that it may be used to react quickly to changing circumstances, is being directed towards imparting the new skills. Continuous training in the industry is rare, and courses are insufficient in number and in quality. Spain has one of the most generous publicly financed continuous training schemes, under which in 1997 about 17 per cent of the 800,000 workers in the sector participated on average in one week's training. Elsewhere, this figure hardly exceeds a few per cent.

A survey carried out in all 15 member countries of the European Union in 1996 showed that 86 per cent of all employees in the hotel and restaurant trade had never received any further training. Exchanging the concepts of skills, capacities and qualification for that of competencies is consonant with the idea of the enterprise as a learning organization in which personnel have enhanced strategic and problem-solving capacities at all levels.

Competencies are described in terms of the results to be achieved, whereas earlier methodologies prescribed tasks, abilities and desired attitudes, leaving the responsibility for the result to the hierarchy. To promote the new concept, the European Working Group on improving training in the tourism industry" convened by the European Commission recommends that research should be undertaken into ways to develop individuals' capacity to make full use of general, technical and personal skills as well as the "soft skills" needed to make use of the other skills, and into how the enterprise can engage and combine the competencies of individuals in an organic manner.

The concept of competencies and their standardization and certification can more easily be introduced where training schemes are flexible. Modular training has always been the basis of training systems in countries where no neat distinction was made between initial training and continuous training. Courses of varying duration, institutional backing, and funding modalities were extended to students of all ages. The new concept of competencies can therefore be introduced speedily to satisfy an increasing need for certification arising from more flexible employment relationships.

Training systems in Costa Rica, the Dominican Republic and Mexico now provide standards for competencies in the hotel, restaurant and tourism sector. Whilst employers offer "earning with learning" to encourage multiskilling, i.e. each acquired competency leads to an increment in salary, trade unions observe that the acquisition of various competencies by workers who occupy jobs outside conventional job classifications tends not to be remunerated appropriately.

Bargaining for appropriate remuneration is more difficult where qualifications are diffuse and do not fit into any pre-established scheme. Moreover, bargaining collectively can hardly take account of all possible individual skill combinations. Indeed continuous training has been far less subject to social dialogue than has initial training.

Where training for competencies has been introduced, standardization and certification of acquired skills are therefore essential. Globalization of the travel and tourism industry and the increased use of e-commerce require a common international understanding and certification of core skills in order to facilitate distance business transactions and assure buyers and sellers that the services they deal with meet certain standards anchored in the qualifications of the labour force.

The competitiveness of small tourism enterprises will increasingly depend on the credibility and reliability of the services they can offer. Hotel and restaurant management training provided by colleges and universities is quite transparent even across national borders, but for operational level workers it is often developed by industry associations of the different sectors involved, and it is difficult to avoid overlapping even at the national level.

In recent years, the certification of skills has also been debated as a means of improving the functioning, transparency and permeability of local and national labour markets. Greater workers' mobility between different employers, seasonal locations and ultimately across borders would enhance human resources allocation and create benefits for all players in the sector. On the other hand, there could be immediate disadvantages for some.

Increased mobility of workers would counteract efforts made by employers to promote in-house human resources development, as the training and incentives provided would not necessarily pay off within the enterprise. Where elaborate initial training systems exist, they are regarded by trade unions as an acquired right. Certification of skills is therefore not endorsed as a substitute for formal initial training (where it exists), but only as a new way of presenting its results.

Greater international recognition of certification is needed where economic integration creates greater mobility within the labour market. In Latin America, an ILO project in the 1990s assisted nine countries on an inventory of qualifications with a view to agreeing on a common classification at a later stage. The European sectoral social partners are considering a proposal to make the description of acquired skills compatible between the European Union countries.

The ECF-IUF and HOTREC are examining the possibility of implementing a "European qualifications passport" for the hotel and restaurant sector. Objections have been voiced on the grounds that certified skills for migrant workers might lead to higher wage claims; however, a qualifications passport could also help employers to find and recruit the right personnel much more easily.

There is a very wide range of private, public and semi-public institutions offering continuous education and training in the HCT sector. In some countries, such as Austria, entrepreneurs are required to obtain an entry certificate to the industry from the public authorities. In Switzerland, this practice has been abolished by most local governments. In these countries, and in others with a strong tradition of public training, the social partners run institutions to deliver continuous training, especially at a higher or middle level.

Although continuous training features frequently in public debate in Austria, only 5 per cent of the workforce had recourse to it in 1996. This may be explained by the reluctance of employers to give workers time for training or to pay for the courses, or it may be caused by the workers' own disinclination to undergo training.

Private hotel and restaurant training facilities are many and varied and employers as well as students tend to criticize the weakness or absence of public or joint (employer/government) control of private training establishments unless they have the authority to issue government-guaranteed certificates. In Switzerland, tight public control is exercised over the six establishments that issue government certificates. Their owners include government, employers' organizations, a workers' organization, a mixed foundation, and a fully private institution.

The remaining 31 private hotel and restaurant schools in Switzerland are not publicly monitored: the Swiss Association of Hotel and Restaurant Schools performs this function. These establishments tend to recruit students from abroad and charge annual fees of up to Sw.frs.20,000. The training provided by the Swiss schools has already assimilated the requirements of the new skills and concentrates on continued general education, languages, and personality skills for managers.

On the technical side, the emphasis is on marketing and product development, while more basic skills are dealt with in training blocks. In the 1960s and 1970s, universities and colleges in the United States were the first to offer hotel and tourism degrees at the tertiary level. Since then, hotel and tourism curricula have been established at college and university level in Germany, Austria and Switzerland.

In Spain, tourism schools used to have agreements with British universities to issue college certificates, but they have now linked up with local universities and their work has been integrated into the official Spanish education system. The training at universities, colleges and generally private specialized schools focuses on management of tourism enterprises or developing tourism destinations and also provides a grounding in both conceptual and practical skills geared to a sector dominated by small and medium-sized enterprises.

The schools are responding to criticism, heard mainly in developing countries, regarding a lack of practical skills in their graduates. In recently industrialized countries, such as Brazil and China, local centres are upgrading their curricula through cooperation with renowned American and European hotel and restaurant schools.

Tourism education and training provided by trade associations is widely available in many industrialized countries. This in general consists of non-degree programmes of a more practical nature. In the United States, as an outstanding example, the Educational Institute of the American Hotel and Motel Association has provided educational services to almost 300,000 persons within the country and elsewhere. The institute offers its own diplomas and certificates in six areas of specialization using textbooks and distance learning materials produced by leading educators from various universities.

Distance training systems with interactive Internet technology and worldwide outreach are starting to operate in all sectors, to the benefit of employees unable to leave work. New work structures require more direct customer contact. Training institutions will accord greater attention to this area which is critical to improvement in productivity.

However, there is little information available about changes in the area of traditional apprenticeships, through which apprentices continue to be trained for the classical occupations of cook or waiter. It is probable, in view of the emphasis on personality and social skills, that training will become less formalized. These changes pose a considerable challenge as regards certification of skills for career purposes.

Elaborate human resource development strategies are usually linked to long-term business development plans, and these are more frequently associated with large enterprises. They are based on a budget set aside for training and providing for trainers to be contracted from outside the hotel. Training budgets can account for up to 3 per cent of a hotel's financial turnover although 1 per cent of payroll is considered substantial.

A system of assessing training requirements through frequent staff appraisal is found at establishments where staff development is taken seriously. Where training is less formalized, on the other hand, it is done by managers or supervisors who are not training specialists; there may be no budget set aside for it in spite of a declared willingness to offer training to staff.

In such cases, training is often reactive rather than proactive, i.e. restricted to induction training for newly recruited staff and statutory (compulsory) safety and health training. It is also common for scheduled training sessions to be cancelled when employees are not replaced at their workplaces and therefore fail to turn up.

Major hotel chains rely largely on their own internal training systems. The Accor Group employs about 140,000 people in 132 countries. Five per cent of staff-related expenditure goes on training in three main areas: initial training for basic qualifications or as an introduction for new employees (delivered in-house); continuous training for director-level employees (department chiefs and others), covering areas such as sales, leadership, customer contacts and so on; and intercultural education.

In-house training at management level generates a strong commitment to the company culture among beneficiaries and yields very high dividends in terms of competitive advantage. In the United Kingdom, a recent survey showed that 60 per cent of all hotels, 53 per cent of restaurants and 70 per cent of pubs and caterers arranged some form of continuous training.

Enterprises employing 11 or more workers provided significantly more continuous training than smaller establishments, as did hotel chains, as opposed to individual, private hotels. This was also the case in Brazil, where research shows that it is generally large or medium-sized hotels that provide training, and that courses are short. Since the larger hotels also tend to offer better employment conditions in other respects too, they can lure workers away from smaller hotels, to the detriment of any staff development policy in the independent hotels.

An example of the way in which some independent hotels address the problem of skills deficiencies is provided by one group of United Kingdom hotels. The group in question has formed a training consortium which works with a regional college to run an employee training and development programme, thus allowing economies of scale. All the hotels in the group can send one or two staff members to attend the courses as required.

Employers use training as a means of curbing staff turnover and of encouraging staff loyalty to the enterprise so as to maintain a core staff. In some cases, training is also given to casual but frequently employed staff who do not want a permanent contract. Training may also be used as a means to make up for difficult working conditions and low remuneration. However, it should be noted that although most workers have received induction training and safety and health training, specific career-building training was generally provided only for a minority of staff, such as those in the upper hierarchy.

The hotel and restaurant industry suffers from a discrepancy between training supply and demand. The specialized training institutions tend to lag behind developments in the industry, and these developments are particularly radical at present. The current skills gap is felt to be at the operational level, whereas training institutions, especially private institutions, are largely geared towards management training. This situation is seen in Brazil, where a study shows that training institutions are relevant only for the higher qualification levels and the majority of staff recruited by enterprises have not undergone any formal training.

Education and training are benefiting from developments in information and communication technologies and are increasingly being delivered through multimedia devices such as interactive on-line connections and CD-ROM. Investments in competitive training packages can be immense: the cost of a recent training CD-ROM for the hotel and restaurant sector was US$1 million. Large chains of hotels are also making use of this technology to fulfil their training needs.

Holiday Inn spent US$2.5 million in 1995 to create online training multimedia for its employees. In 1998, Cendant's Days Inn launched an interactive web-based training programme to maximize the efficiency of the training budget and employee time.

Traditional schools are finding themselves in competition with "cyberschools", and where multimedia training devices are used within traditional schools, teachers are moving away from their traditional role as sources of knowledge towards a new role as "coaches" who help students to tap into much better (electronic) sources of knowledge.

Hotel and restaurant firms are already developing and using multimedia components to guide employees through everything from making a pizza to providing a help desk for night auditors. Students will be able to chose when and where to undergo their training, and to adapt it to their individual learning speed. Education and training will shift from being teacher-centred to being learner-centred.

In the Netherlands, the Hotel School of The Hague has developed an innovative teaching method. There are no traditional classes. Students are set problems individually or in groups and then seek the information they need to solve them, coached by former teachers. In order to do this they have to develop technical and behavioural skills of various kinds and in different areas which hitherto were taught separately.

Students are expected to return to the school throughout their professional life for recycling and "lifelong learning", supported by more or less permanent on-line learning. Increased motivation has been noted both among staff and students. However, performance measurement was harder, and prospective employers will have to adjust their selection criteria in order to assess the new type of training.

Conditions for electronically supported learning are almost ripe for a further "quantum leap". The interconnection of individuals and the formation of virtual learning groups, as well as the ability to call up from a local workstation all the knowledge accumulated by a company or made available through leasing contracts, will change lifelong learning into a continuous updating of personnel.

Tripartite or bipartite cooperation on training policies is common in many countries, at central or local levels. In many countries, developed or developing, staff training is guided by tripartite bodies, some of them sectoral. In Canada, the Hotel Employees and Restaurant Employees International Union (HERE), the Canadian Auto Workers (CAW) and the United Food and Commercial Workers sit beside management on the board of the Canadian Tourism Human Resource Council (CTHRC) which provides labour-oriented input to new certification and training programmes.

The dual system of initial training common in a number of European countries has long been based on a firm consensus between employers' and workers' organizations and on detailed legislation. Proposals for changes in pertinent legislation go through solid consultation procedures before they can be adopted by the competent authorities. Quicker action and intensive consultation is required in the sphere of continuous training, particularly where the improvement of workers' skills is part of a broader strategy for the development of the hotel, catering and tourism sector on a national or regional basis.

Spain provides an example of an effort to rapidly improve the quality of the tourism product in the face of increased international competition. Joint sectoral committees composed of delegates from representative workers' and employers' organizations, technically supported by the Foundation for Continuous Training (FORCEM), appraise training plans with a view to submitting recommendations for public funding to a central (inter-sectoral) joint committee.

The sectoral committees propose certification criteria for continuous training courses in accordance with a national qualification system. Women's training heads the list amongst the target group criteria of the Spanish joint committee on hotels and restaurants. In a number of Latin American countries, tripartite committees on vocational training have been in existence for decades and have influenced some vocational training policies.

However, as most efficient vocational training systems were run by sectoral employers' organizations using payroll-based funding modalities (Brazil, Colombia), unions felt that their participation in steering committees did not always have the desired effect. Designing standards for competencies is a new area in which tripartite cooperation is developing at a rather technical level.

In the European Union, an important step was taken by the ECF-IUF and the European Federation of Contract Catering Organizations (FERCO). In 1999 they concluded an "Agreement on vocational training in the European contract catering sector," which provides for joint initiatives in the area of continuous vocational training.

In particular, it refers to non-discrimination between men and women, full-time and part-time employees and professional categories, in respect of access to continuous training measures. Before the agreement, the ECF-IUF prepared a survey on continuous training in the European contract catering industry based on a questionnaire. It produced a very heterogeneous picture across the countries in terms of regulations (none at all, legislation or collective agreements), volume (in terms of percentage of payroll spent on continuous training), distribution (between blue-collar and white-collar workers), participation of workers' representatives in planning, certification, and other areas.

Social Partners in the hotel and Tourism sector

The social dialogue relationship between the social partners in the hotel, catering and tourism sector in general seems to need more development. Both workers and employers agree that much remains to be done. There are differences, however. Trade unions' concerns are centred on being recognized as partners for social dialogue everywhere.

Employers generally favour greater social responsibility of the enterprise, but not all employers actively promote partnership with trade unions as a means of achieving their social goals. Whatever the current and future shape of partnerships, the understanding of the International Hotel and Restaurant Association (IH&RA) is that the social role of enterprises will be determined by a general trend towards democratization.

Employers also see better partnership between management and labour arising from a common response to the challenges of global competition. They anticipate that workers' organizations will adjust to the discipline that capital markets impose on business, while trade unions are worried by practices such as subcontracting and franchising which they feel create divisions among those working at the same location. They also favour the ratification by ILO member States of the Working Conditions (Hotels and Restaurants) Convention, 1991 (No. 172), and the promotion of equality between women and men at the workplace.

A trend towards improving social partnership can be observed in the Caribbean, where the tourism industry is by far the most important economic sector and where employers' "increasing recognition of the need to engage the cooperation of labour is matched by an increasing recognition on the part of labour that the transformation of business into more productive and competitive operations could mean higher levels of employment and income security".

The coverage by workers' and employers' organizations of the hotel, catering and tourism sector can vary from country to country and from region to region. In general, workers' organizations are more diverse than employers' associations. For historical reasons, trade unions either:

(a) cover a number of sectors, of which the hotel, catering and tourism sector is only one; such is the case of those trade unions that represent the entire food production chain from farms to restaurants or groceries; or

(b) cover a proportion of workers in the hotel, catering and tourism sector as a result of overlapping with their main sectors, such as office workers (travel agencies), transport workers, workers in services in general (France) or in personal services in particular (Austria).

On the other hand, employers' organizations in the HCT sector are more uniform, as hotels and restaurants form a clear majority amongst their membership. As far as the restaurant subsector is concerned, however, representation of employers in a number of countries is subdivided into three different types of specialized organizations covering conventional restaurants, collective or institutional catering, and, more recently, fast-food restaurants, as in Germany.

At the European level, there are two federations of employers' organizations: the Confederation of National Associations of Hotels, Restaurants, Cafés and Similar Establishments in the European Union and European Economic Area (HOTREC), for conventional hotels and restaurants; and the European Federation of Contract Catering organizations (FERCO), for collective or institutional restaurants.

The International Hotel and Restaurant Association (IH&RA) is the largest organization of hotel and restaurant employers at the international level, representing over 750,000 establishments in more than 150 countries. Among its affiliates are some 50 national and international hotel and restaurant chains, many independent hotel operators and restaurateurs, over 110 national hotel and restaurant associations, a number of industry suppliers, and 130 educational institutions in the hotel and restaurant industry.

The largest workers' organization at the international level, the International Union of Food, Agricultural, Hotel, Restaurant, Catering, Tobacco and Allied Workers' Associations (IUF), has 326 affiliated organizations representing 10 million workers in 118 countries. Other international trade secretariats, the International

Transport Workers' Federation (ITF), and Union Network International (UNI), which represents workers in travel agencies, coordinate their action with the IUF.

At the European level, this coordination has resulted in a special European Trade Union Liaison Committee on Tourism (ETLC). Workers in the hospitality sector are in general organized in trade unions to a lesser degree than workers in other sectors. This is due to a number of circumstances including the following:

—The small size of enterprises: Owing to the prevalence of small enterprises, trade union affiliation in the HCT sector may be as little as 10 per cent on average in industrialized countries. However, major hotels in large cities are often unionized, even in countries where smaller units or hotels located outside the centres of large cities are not.

For example, in Canada, an estimated 80 per cent of large full-service down-town and airport hotels were unionized in the mid-1990s. In the United Kingdom, the role of trade unions is stronger in institutional catering, mainly in the public sector, and in a minority of large hotel groups.

— *The mainly young workforce*: Most workers in the HCT sector lack experience with labour issues as they are in their first formal employment, which in most cases is still of a transient nature.

— *High staff turnover*:. Even those workers who stay in the sector will change employers frequently or leave work altogether during certain periods of their life; this is notably the case with women when their children are small.

— *Prevalence of part-time and casual work, irregular hours*: Part-time or on-call arrangements, as well as irregular working hours, keep communication between workers at a low level. In particular, the increasing number of students working in the sector are not necessarily inclined to join trade unions.

— *Varying employment contracts*: Subcontracting, fixed-term employment, and internships in many modern hotel and restaurant enterprises split workers up into several segments with different employment conditions, even when they perform the same tasks. This results in individualization of workers and competition between them.

— *Gender:* Weak affiliation to workers' organizations is more common among women workers since they are disproportionately represented among part-time, casual and young workers and in small enterprises. As they form the less qualified and less well-remunerated segment of the labour force, they also tend to have less access to information and are less able to contribute to workers' collective bargaining power.

— *Attitude factors*: Low self-esteem among the workforce as a collectivity is specific to the hotel and restaurant sector. This is due, firstly, to its generally poor image from which only modern enterprises are immune. The sector is still associated with service in the traditional sense, which involves a "submissive" relationship. Secondly, success in hotel and restaurant services is hard to measure objectively, as it depends on the subjective feelings of customers. The modern customer relationship is built on individual capacities, skills and style, and there is little collective kudos to be had from excellent service.

These factors are reflected in the attitudes of many employers who do not favour the organization of workers in independent bodies with roots outside the enterprise. This is particularly marked in small and medium-sized enterprises and in multinational enterprises whose central management is not used to a trade union culture. Some observers stress the paternalistic management style prevalent in small hotels and restaurants as a factor working against any collective workers' representation.

Trade unions in the hotel and restaurant sector take the view that subcontracting is a method increasingly used to divide workers and thereby weaken collective bargaining power. Moreover, subcontractor enterprises are normally less unionized or belong to a different sector from that of the contracting enterprise.

As a result, they tend to pay lower wages and provide less stable employment conditions. Increasingly, subcontracted services relate to security and surveillance, maintenance, cleaning, catering for hotel personnel and restaurant services for guests. As profit margins are considerably lower for restaurants than for hotel operations, subcontracting of restaurants is being increasingly used in large and medium-sized hotels.

The Hotel Employees and Restaurant Employees International Union (HERE) in the United States and Canada acknowledges that leasing out a hotel restaurant is economically attractive where the hotel is unionized and the leasing enterprise is not. The phenomenon is "exacerbated [for the unions] because in most major

North American cities the restaurant industry is largely non-union".

Trade unions are not opposed to subcontracting in principle but want to negotiate the modalities in order to protect workers against dismissal or deterioration of employment and working conditions. The IUF regards subcontracting as a priority area. Some of HERE's local affiliates bargain to establish joint liability of the employer and the subcontractor.

The franchising system creates similar difficulties with regard to worker representation as subcontracting, especially where legislation provides for company-wide workers' representative bodies based on minimum numbers of employees per unit. Franchised units have the legal status of independent employers, although in terms of their workplace activities they are an integrated part of a larger company.

Trade unions therefore believe that there is an imbalance between the actual size of a company and the legal status of its smaller units. Franchised units benefit from the support of central management in areas such as labour relations, marketing, technological innovation and standardization of procedures. However, agreements concluded between trade unions and companies such as Accor or McDonald's apply only to those units that are owned centrally, not to other franchised units which may well represent the majority of all units, as is the case with McDonald's.

The IUF therefore proposes to its affiliates a strategy aimed at creating the same social conditions for workers in franchised units as for the workers in units fully owned by the multinational company in question, in accordance with the principle "same brand-same rights".

The example of McDonald's is illustrative. By the end of 1999 the McDonald's Corporation employed well over one and a half million workers in.more than 25,000 units in over 110 countries. Some 70-80 per cent of its outlets are franchised, and the company owns 60 per cent of the sites. The actual presence and activity of employees in non-elected workers' participation structures seems to vary considerably depending on the subject dealt with, whether the meeting takes place during working hours, at what time of day, and other factors. Participation is therefore largely on an ad hoc basis.

Collective bargaining in the hotel, catering and tourism sector varies according to the social dialogue culture of a country or region. Collective agreements often differ from each other according to local conditions or enterprise cultures. Trade unionists say that the great variety of collective agreements in the sector may reflect a low level of coordination across geographic and enterprise borders and ultimately follows from low trade union density.

Collective agreements are not yet fully applied to ensure decent working conditions for all and competitive human resource development, even where appropriate clauses are contained in the text. They normally cover mainly remuneration and working conditions, as well as non-discrimination and, more recently, the prohibition of child labour. Training provided by the employer is mentioned only in a minority of collective agreements.

Among the working conditions reflected in most agreements, working time predominates owing to the prevailing irregular working hours and the difficulty of assessing overtime and guaranteeing rest periods. Works councils, where they exist, are often given ad hoc power to agree to changes at short notice.

Remuneration is determined in collective agreements according to occupational group, hierarchical level and personal criteria such as age and seniority. The definition of these criteria often creates difficulties, as classifications of occupations are not generally agreed by the social partners in all countries. Especially in the HCT sector, the definition of occupations is becoming increasingly fluid as phenomena such as multiskilling and flexible distribution of tasks in the enterprise prevail as a result of restructuring and new management methods imposed by competition.

Trade unions are concerned with providing, through collective bargaining, minimum definitions in order to prevent salaries from deteriorating as a result of unclear notions of new work patterns. The classifications of occupations reflected in collective agreements are generally established by bipartite or tripartite bodies, often within the framework of vocational training policies.

The structure and scope of collective bargaining in the HCT sector varies according to legislation and national practice. In North America, Asia and Africa, the workforce of an enterprise tends to be the representative group for the purposes of bargaining. In European countries, on the other hand, negotiations are frequently undertaken on behalf of all workers in the sector or of a subsector on a geographical basis, i.e. at national or regional level.

In Germany, collective agreements with geographical coverage at the regional (Länder) level stipulate minimum regulations and are complemented by collective agreements at the enterprise level. Recently, there has been a tendency to negotiate more issues at the enterprise level than was done in the past in order to take account of sharper differences between the economic performance of individual enterprises.

Chain enterprises may engage in collective bargaining, leaving small and medium-sized enterprises behind; this has been the case in France, where collective agreements were concluded for a number of years for hotel and restaurant chains, while the independent hotels and restaurants adopted the procedure only recently.

As many as 80 per cent of independent (predominantly small) enterprises are covered by the collective agreements, although their workers are normally not unionized. In addition, the collective agreement is regularly extended by Government decree to cover all enterprises and all workers in the sector.

Collective bargaining and collective agreements have been useful in mitigating the negative effects on workers of increased competition between enterprises resulting from globalization, and in preventing an unbalanced distribution between employers and workers of the burden resulting from rapid changes. A common challenge arises when ownership of an enterprise changes.

In such cases, a general clause is sometimes introduced in collective agreements to guarantee the preservation of employment contracts and other arrangements for a certain period. Trade unions have had difficulties in bargaining on the continuity of working and employment conditions in cases where they are faced with a weak local interlocutor and the acting party behind the change is a multinational enterprise based outside the country.

This situation may arise in cases of franchising or in cases of management contracts with strict decentralization of power with regard to labour relations. It is generally the policy of transnational companies to leave labour relations to the local level to ensure that local conditions are taken fully into account.

Trade unions object to this policy, however, where it puts workers in a subsidiary of a multinational enterprise in a less favourable position than other workers of the same chain, or where the mother enterprise's absence from labour relations leaves the local employer in a weak position or unwilling to assume contractual responsibility.

Social dialogue in the hotel, catering and tourism sector does not provide for collective bargaining at the international level at present, apart from agreements concerning the recognition of trade unions and the right of employees to exercise trade union mandates.

Bibliography

Briassoulis, H., "Methodological Issues: Tourism Input-Output Analysis," *Annals of Tourism Research*, 18(2):485-495, 1991.

Cohen, E., "Toward a Sociology of International Tourism," *Social Research*, 39:164-182, 1972.

Doxey, G., "When Enough's Enough: The Natives are Restless in Old Niagara," *Heritage Canada*, 2(2):26-27, 1976.

Dwyer, L., P. Forsyth, J. Madden, and R. Spurr, *Economic Impacts of Inbound Tourism under Different Assumptions, Regarding the Macroeconomy, Current Issues in Tourism*, 3: 325-363, 2000.

Fletcher, J.E., "Input-Output Analysis and Tourism Impact Studies", *Annals of Tourism Research 16*: 514-529, 1989.

Gartner, William C., "Environmental Impacts of Recreational Home Developments", *Annals of Tourism Research 14*: 38-57, 1987.

____________and David W. Lime, *Trends in Outdoor Recreation, Leisure and Tourism*, Wallingford:CABI Publishing (on reserve in Tourism Center), 2000.

Gartner, W. C., *Tourism Development: Principles, Processes, Policies*. New York: Van Nostrand Reinhold, 1996.

Hardin, G., "The Tragedy of the Commons," *Science*, 162:1243-1248, 1968.

Irwin, P., W. Gartner, and C. Phelps, "Mexican-American/ Anglo Cultural Differences as Recreation Style Determinants," *Leisure Studies*, 12:335-348, 1990.

Jafari, J., "Retrospective and Prospective Views on Tourism as Field of Study", *Paper presented at the 1988 Meeting of the Academy of Leisure Sciences,* Indianapolis, Indiana, 1988.

McIntosh, R,. C. Goeldner and B. Ritchie, "*Tourism: Principles, Practices, Philosophies,* 7 th ed. New York: John Wiley and Sons, Inc., 1994.

Murphy, P., "*Tourism: A Community Approach*. New York: Metheun, 1985.

Shanklin, Carol W., "Ecology Age: Implications for the Hospitality and Tourism Industry", *Hospitality Research Journal: The Professional Journal of the Council on Hotel, Restaurant, and Institutional Education, 17* (1), 219-229.

Shanklin, Carol W., Petrillose, Michael J., & Pettay, Amy, "Solid Waste Management in Selected Hotel Chains and Individual Properties", *Hospitality Research Journal: The Professional Journal of the Council on Hotel, Restaurant, and Institutional Education, 15* (1), 59-74, 1991.

Wahab, S., L. Crompton, and L. Rothfield, *Tourism Marketing,* London: Tourism International Press, 1976.

Index